NUGGETS OF WISDOM

Also written by Elsie Spittle

Wisdom for Life

Our True Identity. . . Three Principles

Beyond Imagination—A New Reality Awaits

NUGGETS OF WISDOM

LEARNING TO SEE THEM

Elsie Spittle

Intro's by Barbara Patterson

ISBN-13: 9781519129345
ISBN-10: 1519129343
Library of Congress Control Number: 2015918539
CreateSpace Independent Publishing Platform
North Charleston, South Carolina

First printed in 2015
Printed in the USA

Editor: Jane Tucker
Cover Design: Lynne Robertson
Cover Photo: Andrew Dyer Photography
www.facebook.com/andrewdyerphotography
Author Photo: Lynn Spittle

ABOUT THE AUTHOR

Elsie Spittle has been an internationally recognized trainer and consultant for over four decades. She is in the unique position of having known Sydney Banks, originator of the Three Principles, before he had his epiphany. She witnessed the extraordinary change that occurred in him and the unprecedented impact his work had on hundreds of thousands of people, and how this has brought about a new paradigm in the fields of psychology and psychiatry.

Elsie had the privilege of receiving "on the job" training directly from Mr. Banks, travelling with him to address mental health practitioners, educators, and others seeking a deeper understanding of life. She is considered the first formal teacher of the Principles, after Sydney Banks.

Since then, Elsie has trained executives and employees in the corporate world, and has been instrumental in transforming disadvantaged communities and has worked in juvenile justice settings. She is highly regarded as a public speaker and in her ability to reach the audience, large and small, via a "feeling" that touches the heart and soul. She is sought after for mentoring practitioners. Elsie is co-founder of the Three Principles School, based on Salt Spring Island, BC.

WHAT PEOPLE ARE SAYING ABOUT

Nuggets of Wisdom

"Elsie Spittle is a treasure—warm and wise with a depth of understanding that illuminates human psychology. In her book, *Nuggets of Wisdom,* she shares hundreds of discreet invitations to awaken to our own ultimate resource—the wealth of wisdom within us."
Michael Neill, radio show host and bestselling author of *The Inside-Out Revolution*

"What a beautiful book Elsie has written! I kept being drawn into deep reflection as I read it. Elsie, along with Barb's thoughtful commentary, has crafted a book that speaks directly to your soul. I know this book has the power to really change lives! Please savor these 'nuggets' slowly. Allow them to stir something deep within you, and then wisdom will crack them open to reveal insights that will guide you toward a beautiful life."
Dicken Bettinger, Ed.D. Licensed Psychologist, retired
Founder of 3 Principles Mentoring

"I first came across the work of Sydney Banks and the 3 Principles early in 2013. His discovery has had a profound, positive effect on my life, and on the lives of my co-workers and loved ones. Elsie Spittle has been on this journey with Syd from the very start, and her latest book is a powerful new tool to access these life-changing Principles. The author has drawn from her many years of professional coaching with leading corporate clients, and created a bite-sized way to access one's own deeper wisdom. If you are stuck, or struggling in life, if things are not as you want them to be, then I strongly recommend reading *Nuggets of Wisdom.* You will find it helpful, I can assure you."

James Layfield, CEO, Central Working
One of the 1000 most influential people in London, Tech Ambassador to London, and 2012 Entrepreneur of the Year

"It isn't often I read a book and feel as though I am in the author's presence, being guided to my own wisdom, truth and the deep knowing that lies within all of us, to easily make sense of this life we live.

"The title of this book should be *Everything you ever wanted to know about the Three Principles but were afraid to ask.* Elsie Spittle leaves no questions un-answered with her usual grace, humility and charm. Highly recommended!!!"

Jacquie Forde, CEO, The Wellbeing Alliance,
a non Profit 3 Principles Campaigning and Wellbeing Consultancy

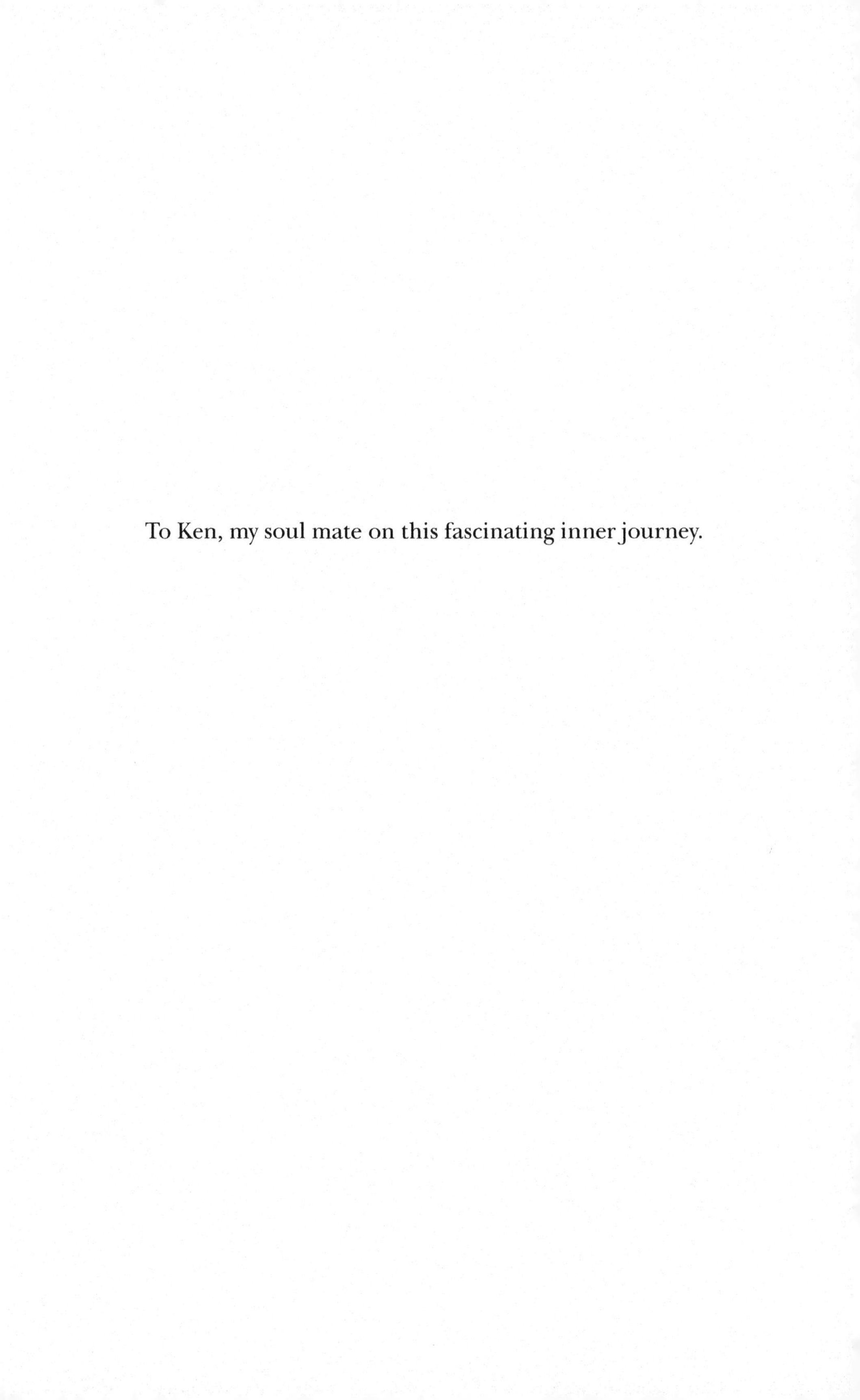

To Ken, my soul mate on this fascinating inner journey.

TABLE OF CONTENTS

INTRODUCTION

MANY READERS WILL be familiar with Sydney Banks' story; how an ordinary working man with minimal education, and no background in psychology or religion, had a spiritual Enlightenment in 1973. So if you want to move on to the Preface, feel free to do so. This introduction is primarily for new readers who may not know about the miracle that happened to Syd. Then again, even readers familiar with the story may find some new information in this overview.

Even now, as I reflect on Syd's story, I am moved by the extraordinary experience that occurred within him in just a few seconds; a few seconds beyond time. The door to a man's soul opened, releasing a limitless bounty of knowledge that would not only transform Syd's life and that of his family and friends, but also create a new paradigm for the fields of psychology and psychiatry.

Imagine for a moment, this ordinary man going about his business; not searching for anything, not knowing there was anything to find. Syd was simply living his life, a sometimes challenging and stressful life, just as countless people do.

Syd emigrated from Scotland when he was in his late twenties. He was a welder; a hard worker, dependable, conscientious, and considered an excellent tradesman. For the most part, he got along well with his work mates, but like anyone, there were some he had issues with.

I know in those days Syd would have liked to have had less stress in his life, but he never entertained the idea that this could be possible. He just thought "Life is what it is, and we do the best we can with the hand we're dealt." I know this because my husband Ken and I were good friends with Syd and his wife, Barb, and we often talked about the problems we had in life.

Syd and Ken worked together in a pulp mill for many years, so they knew each other very well. They shared lunch, often talking about what was wrong with management, how the union could do better for its members, and so on; the grist of the mill in conversation.

At some point at work, Syd noticed a co-worker reading a book, and he became intrigued because the man was so engaged in the content. Syd asked him what he was reading. The man smiled and said, "Oh Scotty, this book isn't for you. You wouldn't understand it."

Syd became even more intrigued and asked to see it so the friend loaned it to him. It was a book by Krishnamurti. He took it home that evening and read it cover to cover. There was something in it that stirred his soul; he didn't know what it was. Nonetheless, Syd's inner world was expanding.

This was exciting to Ken and me as well, and our conversations with Syd and Barb changed to more philosophical ones. When we got together, instead of discussing what was wrong with the world and the latest mishaps at work, we began to consider there might be something deeper going on. We liked that shift in awareness . . . up until several days after Syd had the epiphany that transformed his life. Then, our friendship entered a new phase; a rather unsettling one.

Syd and Barb had gone away to a weekend awareness group, held on another island, which featured a prominent speaker from New York. They had changed their minds about going a few times before actually doing it. One of these times, they had invited us to accompany them, but I was far too frightened to participate, and Ken was just as glad not to attend.

The Banks' did not enjoy their "awareness group" weekend. Syd spoke about this many times in his public talks. They found the sessions negative and confrontational, which prompted a great deal of angst amongst the participants. Barb wanted to leave as soon as possible, but they were dependent on the ferry for travel so had to wait till the next day. Barb decided to rest in their room while Syd went for a walk with another participant.

During that walk Syd and his companion had a very meaningful conversation. They both talked about how insecure they were. At one point, the man told Syd, something along the lines of, *"You're not insecure. You only think you are!"*

As Syd describes it, *"It was like a bomb going off in my head. I heard that insecurity is just thought!"*

I won't attempt to describe what else Syd felt as this is his story and only he can tell it, as he does in a DVD entitled *The Experience*. Suffice to say that after he returned home the next day, he had a deeply mystical experience that revealed to him three spiritual Principles that underlie the human experience; Mind, Consciousness, and Thought.

Syd and Barb came to visit us several days after his profound insight. I was very happy to see them. However, as they settled on the sofa with the cups of tea I'd made them, and Syd began to share what had happened to him, I became increasingly uncomfortable, as did Ken. At one point, Syd said, *"I've found the secret to life. I know what God is and it's not what you think it is."*

Syd knew I had a strong religious background which still had great impact on me, so his words about "knowing what God is" really set off alarm bells in my head. I was very uneasy.

And yet there was something so different about his presence and his appearance. His face was radiant; so much so that it was a little unnerving. I'd peek at him and then look away. And he stood tall, seeming larger than life. I couldn't get this together. He was speaking in a language that I didn't understand; English, yes, but way beyond my comprehension.

What did he mean, "I know what God is"? That's impossible, I thought to myself. Discovered "the secret to life!" Really? What happened to this man?

To make a long story shorter, I'll just say that I resisted Syd's words for well over a year with every fiber of my being. I would invite them to our home with the caveat that Syd not speak about what he'd found. I didn't want to hear about Mind, Consciousness and Thought. It was a lot of mumbo jumbo, as far as I was concerned.

Meanwhile, after his epiphany, Syd returned to work. The dramatic change in his comportment drew attention from his workmates. Syd told us the story of what happened when he opened the door to his locker, to hang up his jacket. He felt a tap on his shoulder, and a voice said, *"What are you doing, going into Scotty's locker?"*

Syd turned around and, seeing his friend, replied, *"It's me; Scotty. Don't you recognize me?"*

The man stepped back in shock, and then as he regained his composure, asked Syd what had happened to him. Thus, curiosity from others about the change in him prompted the unfolding of Syd's service to those around him.

This simple phrase often evokes new learning: *"What happened to you?"*

Syd did share the story of his experience with some of his buddies at work, as well as with some friends. However, he saw that a few were frightened and confused by the change in him, as Ken and I were, so he was very judicious in whom he talked with.

More than anything, it was the level of calmness Syd walked in that drew people to him, as well as the common sense he shared. He wasn't used to being asked for his advice. This was a novel learning for Syd. It was a big change from the anxious, insecure man his work mates were used to. It was an enormous change for Syd himself to see the gift he'd been given via these three spiritual Principles.

What puzzled me was that both Ken and I enjoyed being with the Banks' until, usually at my request, he would share what he'd found that had so dramatically altered his life. They both were happy and enjoying life like I'd never seen them do before. They were fun, carefree; every moment new with potential. Their relationship blossomed to the point where I became jealous and yet yearned for the same quality of tenderness and love in my relationship with Ken.

Inadvertently, I would often find myself asking Syd questions about the change in him. Then I'd get on my high horse when he'd respond.

"I asked you not to talk about this nonsense!" I'd exclaim.

"Well, dearie, you asked me a question."

"Well, I didn't want an answer," I'd say indignantly.

And so it went, until one fateful day, when I was at the height of my resistance. I'd never felt in such low spirits, and wondered what was the point of life. Why was I here? What purpose did I have? And on and on; fruitless thoughts filling my head with angst.

It's amazing how Universal Mind works. The very moment of a crisis of faith in me, questioning my very existence—who comes down my driveway? The Banks'; my happy, wise friends. I couldn't take their presence in my low state of mind, and in my consternation, I hid in the bathroom.

I was frozen with fear, and ashamed that I was hiding from my dear friends. I heard them call *"Elsie"* but I kept still, and then, after a few moments, I heard the front door close. All of a sudden, it felt like a hand lifted me from my hiding place and pushed me toward the door. Opening it, I called out in a shaky voice, *"Here I am. Come in."*

Still distraught, I couldn't invite them to sit down as I busied myself putting the kettle on for tea. Syd came over to me, put his arm around my shoulder, and said in his gentle Scottish brogue, *"You'll be okay, dearie; you'll be okay. You have God within you, as does everyone else on this earth."*

Even as I write this now, I feel emotion welling up within, with the beauty and power of his words. But at that time, his words were the final straw to me. Completely at my wits end, I hastened Syd and Barb out the door, telling them I couldn't take anymore disruption to my life.

As the Banks' drove away, Barb commented to Syd, *"I guess that's the last we'll see of Elsie."*

Syd responded, *"No, Pet, she heard something today."*

"She did? She sure has a funny way of showing it! She just about pushed us out the door."

And Syd was right. Right after they left, I had a brief telephone conversation with a friend, who told me to "listen to myself" because she'd never heard me so upset and so negative. I was completely offended by that and hung up on her. Time slowed and something broke through to my soul, and I had my first insight: "*Thought creates feeling.*" My journey had begun.

I knew in that moment that what Syd was talking about had tremendous potential. He told Ken and me that what he had found would change the fields of psychology and psychiatry, and had the power to alleviate the suffering of the world. I didn't see it fully then; I saw the potential but not the full power.

In the Preface, you will find additional information about what happened to Syd after he left work. I also tell a more complete story about our journey with Syd in my previous books, especially *Beyond Imagination – A New Reality Awaits*, Part One – The Early Days.

In the Epilogue of this book, I share more of what is happening globally as a result of Syd's uncovering of the Three Principles.

PREFACE

My profound, everlasting gratitude goes to the late Sydney Banks, my dear friend and mentor. His unconditional love and patience in helping me *see* beyond the physical realm of experience brought, and continues to bring, insights that shed light on a whole new world, from the inside-out.

Being blessed by the opportunity to travel with Syd, and to witness firsthand how he shared the Three Principles wherever he went, made a lasting impression on me. I saw that whether talking with ordinary people or with professionals from diverse backgrounds, he consistently spoke from the depths of his soul; pure truth that touched everyone he encountered.

My first experience in *seeing* how to share in the business world came about when I accompanied Syd to the home office of the corporation that had employed him for many years. He was invited there after he'd left the mill and moved to Salt Spring Island.

To say that the invitation was unusual doesn't do justice to this unexpected situation. Syd was an ordinary man, who had continued laboring as a tradesman at the pulp mill for ten months after his epiphany; and now here he was, invited to consult with top level executives at the corporate office. How could that be? What drew the executives' interest to meet with a regular workingman, seeking his advice on improving management-employee relations and morale?

His relaxed attitude when we met the vice-president of the division and the head of the human resources department belied the attentive listening he offered to his clients. His calm and kind demeanor set the tone of the meeting and soon everyone was relaxed.

When Syd suggested we continue the meeting at Stanley Park, I must admit my eyebrows shot up in astonishment. Go strolling in the park with executives that Syd had been brought in to "coach"? I'd never heard of such a thing. Feeding peanuts to the squirrels as we wandered the beautiful grounds? Oh my, what was he thinking!

Yet the results were astounding. At the end of the day, the executives were so lighthearted and enthused with what they were *seeing* inside themselves; their wisdom come to life revealing insights that helped them in their work.

Syd was very pleased with the outcome of this profound and practical get-together. He was invited back and although he was honored at their request, he felt it would be good for me to go instead, and asked that I follow up with them, which I did.

To be quite candid, when I attended their two day team retreat, I felt out of my depth, and found myself listening intently, trying to make sense of the content of their meeting. Listening was the only thing I knew how to do.

What I discovered was that although I was listening to the details of their team development strategizing, I did pick up pertinent information via the tone that was present during their discussion. I could "feel" when they were listening to one another, and when the tone was off to the extent that their conversation was no longer productive.

It surprised me that they seemed unaware of the difference in tone and just continued to plow ahead, with mounting frustration. Finally, when the vice-president asked what I thought, the only thing that came to mind was to offer my observation about how the positive tone brought out the best in the team, and the reversal: that when the tone was off, people shut off from one another, and the result was non-productive or worse.

This seemed to make sense to some of the team and the meeting progressed in a more positive way.

I learned two important lessons in my first entry into the business world. First of all, the importance and value of listening, and secondly, the relevance of the tone/feeling of engagement. These two things continue to play out in life generally, as well as in business and other areas of endeavor.

To sum it up, I learned to *see* in a situation where I was so out of my depth that I felt I had no choice other than to be still and listen. Wisdom came to my rescue and provided very helpful answers that prompted the team to work in a more constructive manner. Such a simple response: Listen and be consciousness of the feeling.

SYDNEY BANKS EXCERPT

"It's nothing new. It's something that's been on this reality since the beginning of time and it's called Truth. And Truth is a spiritual intelligence before the formation of this reality we know.

How do you get to this Truth? How does it become alive? It's really very simple. The Three Principles that bring everything into creation... Divine Mind, Divine Consciousness and Divine Thought. And with Mind, Consciousness and Thought to guide you through life, you learn to use them properly.

Now you don't really have to think about Mind because Mind is the intelligence of all things. You've already got it. Consciousness makes you aware. You're already aware. What's left is Thought and Thought is like the rudder of a ship; it guides you through life. And if you can learn to use that rudder properly, you can guide your way through life way, way better than you ever imagined.

You can go from one reality to another. You can find your happiness. And when illusionary sadness comes from memories, you don't try to figure them out, please don't try and do that, you'll get yourself in trouble. All you have to do is, simplicity again, is realize that it is Thought. The second you realize it's thought it's gone. You're back to the now, you're back to happiness.

So, don't get caught up in a lot of details. In this world, the smaller it is the more powerful it is. And here we have Mind, Consciousness and Thought. That's very simple. That's the answer."

-Sydney Banks 2000

FOREWORD BY BARBARA PATTERSON

We were on Salt Spring visiting over a cup of coffee when Elsie invited me to work with her on this book. I knew instantly my answer was "Yes." What I didn't know was how I could be of any help. What did I have to give? I've never written a book. However, in her offer, I could feel a deeper invitation. An invitation to step into the unknown, to follow wisdom and inspiration without knowing where it would take me. To know that "Yes" was all I needed to know.

It's striking to me how one moment the world looks one way and in an instant, all of a sudden new possibility and opportunity emerge. This is one small example of the hope and potential that understanding the Three Principles has given me.

Elsie explained that over a number of years she kept notes from her sessions with clients and told me her vision for creating a book where she could share the insights that emerged from those conversations. I was thrilled to have a chance to see the exchange between her and her clients. Being fairly new to this work and understanding, I was an eager sponge.

That night I began reading and I was immediately struck by the depth, the simplicity, the practical and profound insights and wisdom that came through Elsie and her clients. Over breakfast the next morning, I couldn't stop talking about what I was seeing and what reading these nuggets of wisdom woke up inside of me.

As I read and allowed the words to wash over me, I had personal insights and experienced my level of consciousness shifting in a really beautiful way. Another nice surprise was that I was learning a ton about teaching the Principles by reading these. For instance, I realized that it didn't matter who was in front of Elsie; whether an executive, manager, coach or parent, she spoke the truth of the Principles unapologetically and while they may not have always understood her, the "feeling" kept them coming back for more. They were engaged in the learning.

These nuggets highlight people's natural ability to see depth; that ultimately Elsie was making visible what they already knew to be true but may not have seen yet. . . their own wisdom. When we look in the direction of our innate well-being or our true nature, anything is possible.

The following pages are full of real-world insights that came forward in those sessions. Many are in the language of her clients, using examples from their lives. I love that Elsie chooses not to "doctor" or change the language so it is grammatically correct, but instead chooses to leave it as the client said it. It shows the purity of their insights happening in a meaningful way for them.

These simple statements or nuggets stand on their own and often when reading one of them, I would experience a quiet reflective state and/or a moment of clarity and new sight. I invite you to let these simple and profound truths wash over you. Notice what strikes you, what resonates with you, what wakes up inside of you.

I was and continue to be inspired by the power of what emerges when we get together in conversation with others looking in the direction of the Principles. I am confident that anyone who reads this will have their own journey of insights and deeper learning.

I'm forever grateful to Elsie for the invitation to work with her in this endeavour and for her incredibly generous spirit in sharing her stories, her knowledge and her wisdom with all of us.

Enjoy!

Barbara Patterson

AUTHOR'S NOTE

Sydney Banks' book, *The Missing Link, Reflections on Philosophy & Spirit,* has long been one of my favorite books, and I decided I'd like the format of my book to be similar. To be a reflective book that draws the reader in toward their own wisdom.

The nuggets of wisdom contained in this book are primarily my teaching points shared on client calls. The nuggets that I've included from my clients are largely unedited, as I want the real conversation to stand on its own merits, faulty grammar and all. I want to highlight the wisdom that emerged from all the people I spoke with who revealed their innermost thoughts and insights. I have such respect for them, unafraid to share their vulnerability in their dedication to learning more about life, relationships and leadership.

The clients' insights and my own words are not differentiated in any way; this is intentional.

From the beginning of these conversations several years ago, I felt I wanted to save them. I had a sense that the nuggets would be as helpful to others as they were to my clients and to me. The truth in them sparked something deeper that helped us continue our learning.

As I've gone through the book, letting the material guide me on how best to present the content, the word "seeing" was prominent throughout. It struck me that *seeing* is the operative word for change, in regard to leadership, relationships or simply living in mental health. The simplicity of *seeing* levels the playing field of life. There is nothing to do, nothing to stress about; the gift of *seeing* comes from our true nature, our spiritual birthright.

A question I've been asked many times is, "How does one introduce the Principles to the business world?" Often there is an underlying concern that, in business, it's not appropriate to talk about matters that are labeled "spiritual." My guide in this situation is to follow the feeling of when it's appropriate and when it's not. The feeling of wisdom will guide.

With simplicity, I introduce the Principles as the spiritual creative intelligence behind life. I can't recall that I've ever had an adverse reaction. Part of this is because under our various disguises, we're all the same spiritual energy and somewhere we *know* this. It's this *knowing* that I speak to, not the disguise.

My inspiration in being true to what I *know* comes from Sydney Banks. He never hesitated in sharing the Principles in their purest form, to whomever he was speaking. I do my best to follow his example and to share with love and understanding.

Read this book for pleasure; let it speak to your wisdom so you can *see* how much you know. Enjoy! Reflect! Live to the fullest!

Valuable nuggets ahead. . . Proceed slowly. Read 1 – 2 nuggets, pause, reflect, and then close book. Repeat as needed. You don't want to read this like a regular book; you want to take your time with it. Digest it. Savor it. *See* it.

THE THREE PRINCIPLES

BARB'S INTRO TO THE THREE PRINCIPLES

WHAT STANDS OUT for me as I read this section is the simplicity in which Elsie and her clients talk about the Principles. While the language or words may shift a little based on what's relevant for them, it all leads to the same place. The power of Mind, Consciousness and Thought and the role they play in creating our moment-to-moment experience of life; bringing the formless spiritual nature of life into the form of our personal reality. Elsie gently brings each person's awareness back to the ROLE of Thought, Consciousness and Mind and as a result they have simple and profound insights that are meaningful for whatever is happening in their life.

I know for myself and many others I've taught or spoken to, it's common when we first come across the Principles to focus too much on the form of our understanding and how it shows up in our teaching, work with clients and/or helping us have a better life. As I read these nuggets it reminds me to go deeper. Focus instead on understanding how the gift of Consciousness along with Mind and Thought allows us to experience life at infinite levels of understanding. This is good news! This is where the hope and potential of the Principles lives—that we have infinite possibilities to experience ourselves, our lives, as new/fresh in any given moment.

Throughout this section and the book, Elsie talks about "noticing" or "seeing". This really resonates with me. Noticing is powerful. Noticing is enough. The moment we notice, we are more present and awake than we were just a second ago. And that's all it takes for momentum to begin shifting in a new direction. Our level of consciousness has already shifted. There is nothing else to do—it's already done. As Elsie says, 'notice—then stop looking'.

Finally, as a practitioner, it is reassuring and touching to see how in the freshness of the moment, Elsie and her clients are building off of each other, and the phrasing and language take shape in a meaningful way for the client. To me this is a perfect example of the power of keeping it simple. Show up, be present, and listen deeply to the client and go wherever it makes sense. Our own wisdom will come forward and guide us and will allow us to build on what the person before us presents.

THE THREE PRINCIPLES

The Three Principles are the spiritual energy behind life.

- Mind - the primary intelligence before form, more than the intellect; where wisdom comes from.
- Consciousness - the awareness of life, that we are the "thinker" and create our own experience.
- Thought - the power that humans have to create experience.

These three gifts, together, underlie human behavior. Use them wisely.

Another way to describe the Principles:

- Mind - the spiritual energy of everything, both form and formless.
- Consciousness - our awareness of who and what we really are.
- Thought - the gift we have to think and create our moment to moment experience, using the spiritual energy that we are part of.

The more deeply we understand the Principles, the more we are able to sustain feelings of well-being. We call them Principles because they are foundational to the human experience and apply to everyone and are within everyone.

The more we see the Three Principles in action, the more perspective we gain. i.e. Noticing how your emotions/behaviors affect others = Consciousness. The insights you get when mowing the lawn, planting flowers = Mind. Creation of experience/behavior = Thought. In other words, this is evidence that the Principles are at work within you. When you use them effectively, you manufacture a healthier environment. When you use them less effectively, you manufacture a less healthy environment.

Consider the nature of the Principles rather than what the Principles do. Look at what the Principles *are*—formless intelligent energy that humans use to guide and find Self.

See the nature of Principles as spiritual, before form. What the Principles do, create experience, is form. Just considering the formless nature deepens our feeling and therefore our understanding.

Form = function; Formless = energy, power behind form. *See* what is illusion and what is reality. *See* that reality changes as thought changes. Therefore, what we think of as reality is illusion.

Demystifying the Principles actually brings them more to life in a simple, practical and spiritual way. Wisdom is more attainable when you realize this.

The more we see how the Principles underlie the human experience, the more "habitual" healthy thinking becomes, because innate health is our default setting.

Connect Mind and Consciousness more in your everyday experiences, just as you have Thought. You talk about insights; know they come from Mind. You talk about being aware of your feelings; know that awareness is Consciousness. We use Thought to create experience.

It's important for people to have some understanding that Consciousness (awareness) and Mind (where insights come from) are part of the equation along with Thought, in order to gain insights about their thinking without getting attached to their thinking. Knowing that M/C/T = our R (reality) explains and completes the action.

Math is pure science. Math = form in numbers yet there is infinity in "pi"—goes on forever. Three Principles is pure science yet there is infinity in pure energy—goes on forever.

The Three Principles understanding is not problem oriented; rather it points to the innate mental health or wisdom in all individuals. When an individual accesses more wisdom, the problems begin to be resolved.

You can count on the Three Principles of Mind, Consciousness, and Thought. They are part of us, whether we know it or not. They allow us to create our experience, both healthy and unhealthy. Knowing how they work gives us perspective and puts us in charge of our experience.

MIND

What is valuable to know is that Universal Mind and personal mind are both the same energy, used in two different ways. Universal Mind is pure energy, the energy behind life. Personal mind is the intellect, already formed. Both can work in partnership, when the personal mind understands this fact.

Universal Mind is the source of both form and formlessness. It draws us inward; It is us, and we are It. The more we realize that, the less duality there is.

Even though we don't understand the formless, just considering this can take us deeper.

Understand that creativity and insights come from Mind. The doors of understanding open when our personal thinking slows down to the "quiet mind" state.

See how Mind expresses itself more fully in the moment, in the most practical way; technical strategies, business plans, etc. *See* this as the partnership between the formless and form.

Universal Mind is like the parent. It nudges us or kicks us in the pants when we get off track.

See the power of the human/spirit—know perseverance and determination come from Universal Mind.

Coincidence and connectedness directly relates to being in the moment and Universal Mind.

In the moment = union with Self (Universal Mind).

CONSCIOUSNESS

Doing without doing; learning to just BE without doing activities to get somewhere higher in consciousness. Trying to "do" something means that we don't already HAVE higher consciousness! Doing gets in the way.

Another aspect of Consciousness—*noticing* the noise in your head. The *noticing* is the job being done. There is nothing to do to grow in wisdom, except notice you are the thinker.

Notice—then stop looking—the job is done!

See the value of noticing thinking rather than examining thoughts. Just noticing is Consciousness in action. Examining thinking is examining content and is of no value; it just gets us more involved in unhealthy thinking. *Noticing* is operating from Principle and neutralizes our unhealthy thinking.

When one is out of integrity with inner wisdom, frustration occurs. Frustration is the sandpaper effect of Consciousness! It rubs away the cloudy surface revealing the inner beauty.

Consciousness plays its role by helping us become more aware and sensitive to the feelings/tone of the situation, i.e. Group of angry people in car park, we experience flight/fight syndrome. Consciousness will help us identify the energy/feelings coming from group as dangerous or simply people talking together.

Recognizing when not in healthy state of mind is Consciousness in action.

Notice how much more aware you are and acknowledge that is Consciousness at work. The more you *see* this, the more Consciousness thrives.

Creativity: exploring how to get there, *seeing* that the first step is to nurture a quiet mind. Sometimes it feels like we have to force ourselves to be still, then the mind opens to new insights. Recognizing the need for quiet/creativity is Consciousness in action.

Consciousness neutralizes unhealthy emotions. This is very important to know as this lessens judgment of yourself and others, and helps sustain well-being.

Learn to slide up and down levels of understanding, see them as "different" levels of understanding rather than "low or high." *See* what you can learn when you are in different levels. Don't judge them as low just as you don't judge the tide for being a low tide. *See* as natural and that low tide allows you to see a great distance and to see different things that weren't visible when the water covered the sand.

Instead of digging into details, we're flying above the fray and seeing clearly how to handle the situation.

Realizing = Consciousness. It is realizing that we are "out of it" that allows our thinking to shift. Again, it's not about time, it's about state of mind and being aware.

Catching yourself after a situation occurs and realizing (Consciousness) that you could have done it differently is wonderful progress.

Appreciate the fact that you are *noticing* your responses quicker. The more you notice this action, the more it will happen. This is significant as it shows you are moving into the driver's seat of creating your experience, rather than being a passenger.

Acknowledging the change in your level of calmness and state of mind helps prolong your healthy functioning.

Excellent! Noticing (Consciousness) that when you are more relaxed, clearer thinking and deeper awareness happen.

Life is a classroom and gives us assignments. i.e. Noticing moods and not liking the feeling. Noticing moods = Consciousness in action. I don't like it = personal thinking. Be grateful you noticed. You decide what you want to focus on.

Realize that sensitivity happens because our level of Consciousness or understanding is heightened. Less personal thinking is cluttering the mind, which allows deeper Consciousness to be accessed.

What is the difference between examining your thinking versus knowing that you will deal with it in your own time? i.e. "Splinter in eye" is Consciousness prompting us to deal with what we need to in order to move ahead. There is ease in knowing that we all have our own pace. Consciousness won't let us forget, so we can relax and let things unfold.

"Blinders on and grinding"—the gut feels something is off. This is Consciousness trying to get our attention that we're off balance. Wonderful! Helpful insight!

"Noticing edginess" is Consciousness in action. When you notice edginess, that means you had to slow down for a moment in order to have noticed it. That is excellent.

"Don't see it until we see it"—relates to how the Principles work—our thoughts create our reality. When we calm down, we can *see* it. When we're stressed, we can't see.

See the difference between Universal Consciousness and personal consciousness. Once you have an insight, it's your consciousness that has increased. Universal Consciousness is the Oneness that we're all part of and where that insight was born.

Used to think that *seeing* our poor behavior when we were in lower levels of consciousness meant that we were sinking fast, rather than *seeing* is a gift, a blessing, Consciousness in action.

THOUGHT

Be aware of how many times you say "but." Know that "but" keeps you where you are and doesn't let in new ideas. That is how Thought works via our free will. When we say "but" our reality doesn't change.

You are the thinker, period! Understanding this gives perspective and clear thinking, allowing insights to happen which give you the answer to the situation.

See that Thought is the bridge between the nature of the Principles and our experience. *See* that we have the power of Thought to create our experience.

Our assumptions (thoughts) create the feeling of insecurity and security.

Seeing the role of Thought helps us get past the "story" we make up.

Tone of thoughts creates tone of voice, body language. Change tone of thoughts, body language, etc. changes automatically.

Recognizing negative emotions is all you need do; unnecessary to examine "why." Realizing that it's all thought brings a shift in understanding.

Focus on the fact that you are the "thinker" and not so much on what you are thinking about. Examining our personal thinking takes us away from the principle of Thought and gets us stuck in the content of thought.

What is the difference between wishful thinking and insightful thinking? Gaining more understanding of the role of Thought yields a clear mind which then offers insights rather than relying on personal wishful thinking which comes from the intellect.

Where does intention come from? Intention is a thought, which we use to create experience. Points back to the Principles.

See that bad experiences with others will prompt us to proceed with caution in future interactions with them. However, if we have a poor experience with a team, i.e. our favourite team losing—we still love to go to their games. Or if we buy a pair of shoes too tight, that doesn't prevent us from loving shopping! So somewhere in there, our experience in sports/shopping remain more neutral than the past experiences. Could this be our thinking about the subject???

Thought is neutral, with no power other than what we give by our attention. If we let thoughts flow, which is the nature of Thought, they do not cause any harm.

Interesting to see how we create our story, "This is OK," "I'm alright," while we're mentally asleep to our deeper wisdom. With the power of Thought we can create anything we want and it appears logical. Underneath the logic lies Truth and it does not sleep.

What changed for you as you began to realize the power of Thought? Realized responsible for own experience and for own feelings; that circumstances are not responsible but the way one thinks about the situation is key.

See how we build our story by sometimes using Thought against ourselves. Then insight occurs and provides some clarity. We realize how lucky we are to be able to pull back from stress, to mentor other leaders, and to focus on other things that need doing; to have a life outside of work.

Events happen—how we *think* about them is what makes the difference in how we will experience them.

Keep in mind when you have thoughts like "Things will go back to the way they always were" your thoughts help make it so. Don't forget, thoughts create our experience in life. Therefore if we think something is so, it is that way. If you think people won't change for good, they won't, in your experience.

LEARNING TO SEE

BARB'S INTRO TO LEARNING TO SEE

Do I want to live a guided life? Do I want to create my life from a place of wisdom, deeper intelligence, or from my wants, my drive, my fears or my ideas about "playing big"?

Ultimately, this decision was a pivotal one for me. As I read through this section, I am reminded again and again of this choice. And often I have to remind myself that I no longer want to create my work or my life from my old paradigm of self-improvement, push and striving. I'm interested in creating from the infinite potential and possibility that lies within us; the infinite well of creative potential and connection that is our birthright and available for us all.

In many ways, I relate to the insights Elsie and her clients share on quiet mind, being in the moment, understanding, wisdom, and the unknown. As I began to see that there was another way to create and live my life, I saw the relationship between a quiet mind and my ability to hear beyond the noise of my thinking to my deeper truth—my wisdom. I began to see how much I was living in my head, thinking about my life and the future, versus being present to whatever was in front of me. This means I was living an internal life versus living life. Thinking about my life was not the same as living life.

As with Elsie and her clients, my insights came to life for me in a similar way. My natural learning curve took over. Over time, as my mind quieted, I got present and engaged in life in a more powerful way. I was getting more "filled-up" by life; experiencing its richness, feeling more connected to others. I heard my wisdom more and I saw more potential/ new ideas. Things seemed to fall into my lap. Not surprisingly, when I look at the moment with a quiet mind or a free mind, I see more and therefore I experience more possibility and potential. It makes sense but it took me a while to catch on.

I get impatient, I buy into my fearful or insecure thoughts at times or I get lost, but as Elsie so clearly shows us throughout—we will always wake up to our truth. Consciousness helps us wake up to our truth. Again, nothing to do, we can rest in the certainty that wisdom, insight, and clarity will emerge. As with each of her clients, our wisdom informs our lives and comes forward when we need it. "Listen to your own wisdom more."

QUIET MIND

REFLECT ON THE value of a quiet mind; no matter if it's a result of porch rocking, mowing the lawn, listening to music. The mind, without the distraction of busy thinking, allows wisdom to be released. The quiet mind is where insights occur. Quiet mind is productive and efficient, and offers more clarity, understanding, and creative ideas.

Quiet mind is <u>before</u> the brain just like wisdom is <u>before</u> the thinking process. Quiet mind and wisdom are formless. Thinking process and brain is form.

How to stay focused on having respectful relationships? Cultivate a quiet mind!

Understanding that we are the "thinker" and have innate mental health as our default setting brings a quiet mind.

Don't look for blame; look for resolution, from a calm state of mind.

Go inside, where your quiet strength is strongest. This is where your protection from the craziness of the world resides.

When we're in a quiet mind state, our wisdom is active and ready to respond in the most appropriate way.

There is safety in being quiet when others are reactive. Quiet defuses the situation, rather than adding fuel to the flame.

FEELINGS

When transitioning in life situations, it's helpful to recognize "good moments" and to see that the good moments come with feelings of gratitude. This keeps well-being alive.

See the power of profound feelings becoming the educator. Deep feelings draw out insights from within each individual to transform and improve life.

Connecting to your essence through deep feelings offer protection and comfort via insight.

It's not about being "right"; it's about keeping the feeling positive. From a positive feeling, you can see clearly and do what needs to be done. Often times, just trusting that innate health in yourself and others will ultimately guide you and things will turn out better than you could have imagined.

The difference between being the observer and being gripped by thinking is the quality of feeling. If feeling frustrated, impatient, stressed, that is a signal that you need to slow down, take a mental breather and wait for wisdom to emerge.

Trust the feeling of wisdom; the feeling will always lead us home because the feeling is wisdom before form. The intellect is from data/memory which is already formed. The intellect grasps details and gets skewed. Wisdom is simple and clear.

How can you tell the difference between opinion and insight? By the feeling.

Knowing that our thoughts create our feelings is empowering. This knowledge allows our wisdom to emerge more of the time.

Realizing that thoughts create feelings helps defuse the feelings when they are negative, and enhances the feelings when they are positive.

Monitor the tone/feeling of decisions; feelings are the educator. Positive feelings tell you you're on track, negative feelings tell you to slow down and look again.

Listen to the feeling. Negative thoughts create negative feelings. It's your choice to entertain them or let them go.

Trust the feeling of wisdom and that it will always guide you on what to do; remember, nothing is written in stone. It's all Thought! Change the thought and life changes.

MOODS

It's good to be able to acknowledge when we're in a low mood. It helps put it in perspective and adds a dose of humility. The beauty is that being able to acknowledge this means that we're already moved past the low mood.

Be grateful for *seeing* that we're gripped. It's so much better than being annoyed or judging ourselves because we're in a low mood.

Thinking low thoughts creates the low mood; don't focus on what those thoughts are. That makes it worse because you are examining the form. Just *see* that you are in a low mood and be grateful for seeing.

See that feelings/emotions are psychological tools that tell us when our thinking is off track. When we're feeling bad, we're having negative thoughts; it's helpful to see that.

See emotions as neutral, as signposts that alert us to the quality of our thinking and helps keep us on track.

When you *see* unpleasant feelings with neutrality, it helps defuse the situation. It may not terminate them immediately but it lessens the intensity so you become more the observer rather than the victim.

Keep in mind that if your emotions are negative and unhealthy, you want to stop, look, and listen. Impatience, stress, anger, etc. are telling us to slow down and keep calm. Calm tells us we're heading in the right direction.

Be grateful when you notice a low mood. This gratefulness helps defuse the low mood because you can't be upset and grateful at the same time.

When heading "south" (low mood), it's helpful to know that life is a contact sport and to understand that we will not stay in peak feelings all the time.

See that even though we head south, we don't stay as long and we respond differently. This is invaluable; it helps us move back to a healthier mental climate sooner. If we fight it and feel guilty or disappointed, those thought/feelings will keep us gripped longer.

It's unnecessary to figure out why/how we shift from one mood to another. It's like "trying" to be calm....Trust that at some point, the penny will drop, insight will occur, and you'll just *see* why. Meanwhile, enjoy the fact that you notice the shift.

UNDERSTANDING

A SHIFT IN understanding can be so subtle that we may not even notice that we are living our everyday life in a different state of mind. This becomes more profound upon reflection; a perfect blend of the ordinary and extraordinary.

When you "sense" something, i.e. nature of the Principles, that sense is deeper understanding. Sensing is a degree of knowing.

Knowing is a shift in one's level of understanding that cracks open the door of beliefs, and brings insight beyond habits of thought.

Opportunities always come to those who are open to what life has to offer. Your new understanding puts you in the path of opportunity.

It is very helpful to notice the change in yourself because it reinforces that your understanding of the Principles is more effective and adds to your feeling of well-being.

When life throws us a curve ball or two, it provides us with opportunity to go deeper into our understanding of the role of the Principles in creating the human experience.

Higher quality of time/thinking comes from a shift in your level of understanding. This is a psychological fact. Thought comes first; it is fundamental. That is why it's considered a Principle.

Challenges present an opportunity to move to another plateau (level) of understanding. This is how mental evolution takes places and is meant to be appreciated.

Listen for wisdom versus listening for understanding. Listening for wisdom provides a flavor of health whereas listening for understanding can sometimes move into content of thought.

WISDOM

What is wisdom? Is it based on education, experience, age? Interesting what people think about this. Stating that wisdom is innate is a new idea to many people. Though people experience it naturally they may not be sure what it is: i.e. woman was rear-ended by another car, was prepared to haul off and yell at the driver until she got out of her vehicle and her eyeballs met his belly button. Wisdom quickly came to the rescue and she held her tongue! She didn't realize that was wisdom. She just took it for granted.

Everyone has innate wisdom. We never lose it, although it may be covered by our erroneous thinking. Nonetheless, when we calm down, and even when we don't calm down, it is always ready and waiting to be released.

The wisdom we are exploring is innate to everyone. There are different names for it: common sense, intuition, knowing. It is where insights come from, and how we learn, from the inside out.

Living in wisdom has far reaching implications. When people see that we don't react to challenging situations as much as we did before, it is hopeful to them, it evokes curiosity, and it calms them down. This in turns spreads out to whoever they meet and on it goes.

See beyond someone being "worked up." Wisdom has many disguises. Sometimes when someone gets worked up, they may be open to help. Wisdom's wake-up call can disturb and will release knowledge.

Understanding the Principles expands our ability to live life to the fullest. In other words, understanding "supersizes wisdom and time."

We become our own best teacher, knowing that when we slow down and open up, we hear wisdom.

Wisdom is knocking—the struggle comes from our ego not listening to wisdom.

Acknowledge your own wisdom. Cherish it and take time to listen to yourself.

Consider not asking "why" so much and know that wisdom, when allowed, will provide the answer. i.e. "Why did that bother me?" Suggest you simply acknowledge "That bothered me." Acknowledgement moves you past analysis to insight, which comes from wisdom.

Wisdom speaks to each individual in a way that is appropriate and specific to that individual.

Spiritual exploration is wonderful, particularly when we allow space for our own wisdom/insights to emerge rather than getting too much content from others.

Seeing that going inside and releasing our own wisdom, in silence, is the best help there is.

Wisdom is released from within, rather than gathered from outside of ourselves.

Don't look for outcome. When you realize something, trust that your intellect will catch up with your wisdom. When the time comes, something spontaneous will occur that will help improve your relationship with others.

Listen to your wisdom. It is coaching you; you just want to listen to it more.

See that wisdom guides us always, if we allow it to. i.e. if it doesn't feel right, don't do it.

INSIGHT

Insight is available in every human being. As you start to consider this, insights are released and soon you are living a healthier, more productive life, and helping others with their lives.

The Three Principles learning is not memory based, rather it is insight based. The value of insights is that we never lose them; they are always ours, even when we don't always live what we've learned.

Looking for insights to happen prevents them from occurring.

Insights will tell you, at some point, what beliefs got in your way. When you try to figure it out with personal analysis, this puts up a barrier to clear thinking/insights.

Insight "shorted out" the depression. i.e. Story of the woman who was so caught up in her thinking and asked, "What will be left if I stop my thinking?" The response was "Peace."

"Less thought" is easier to maintain. This shows that personal thought is lessening and insightful thought is taking its place.

The world of insight is more readily available, more subtle, more every day; not always big dramatic insights.

Insight = spark of divinity.

Insight/wisdom is *before* the thinking process.

People want instant gratification rather than being thankful for the insights they have had. This desire gets in the way of more insights.

LEARNING

DON'T BE SIDE tracked by your personal thinking. Realize that every opportunity to extend yourself into something new is an opportunity for growth.

Focus on what you *do* know, not what you don't know. Otherwise you're always looking for more, discontent with what you have already learned.

Be more the observer rather than getting too engaged in unhealthy thoughts and behavior. In this way, even when you're going through some unpleasantness, you aren't as engaged and the feelings aren't as intense. Also it doesn't last as long; consequently, less stress. Yes, being the "observer" is very helpful.

Taking "responsibility" for creating our experience in life used to look like a burden. Now it's seen as a "gift." This responsibility means we have choice over our experience, no matter what goes on. It's how we *see* it that matters.

"Let the game come to me" (let the learning come to me) is a great philosophy to live by; going with the flow. Let go of being the seeker—be a learner.

See how life puts situations in front of us giving us the opportunity to learn, i.e. struggles with people who don't listen or are opinionated. Learning that it always comes back to "me" and how I think about the situation.

"Once a mind is stretched, it never reverts to previous state." (Paraphrasing Chief Justice Oliver Wendell Holmes, Jr.)

See that your experience of feeling out of control is a gift, a wake-up call to move forward in your understanding. The fact that you *saw* this means you had a "shift."

Appreciate the "blips" of life. *See* as life's assignment/life's classroom.

Don't have the "yippee" frenetic energy quality anymore; more of a calm, learning feeling. This is progress!

We all have our own pace in learning. i.e. man forgiving his mother for the wrongs she had done to him, several years after she died. In forgiving her, he forgave himself as well. He realized that at the time, they were both doing what made sense to them, given their state of mind.

UNKNOWN

Taking a step into the unknown, with faith, moves us into the future of what we feel we are destined to do, without really knowing how. With a leap of faith, certainty comes and the path becomes clear.

Stepping into the unknown has taken on a different feeling. Rather than fear or uncertainty, there is a feeling of embracing the unknown. This is because you are so comfortable and at peace in the moment. The role of the Principles is brought into focus, offering more guidance as to what is most appropriate in the moment.

Our thinking about the unknown can create insecurity. However, look at it this way; when we receive a gift, which is unknown, that's okay. We're comfortable and delighted. It's nice to have the same feeling when the unknown comes along in work/life. When you think about it, we never really know what will happen. Life is "unknown."

See more about the "gift" of the unknown and realize that it isn't about making right or wrong decisions; rather it is the ability to make decisions that is the gift.

GRATITUDE/LOVE

Continue to "manufacture" a healthy environment and appreciate the results, without hoping for more. Hoping for more gets in the way of appreciating what you have now.

Power of love gives us strength and helps move us past mental and physical frailties.

Be grateful that you are wiser now than you were 6 months ago. Gratitude is a short-cut to well-being.

Gratitude opens the door to new insights and deeper feelings.

The best way to move deeper into understanding human nature is via gratitude; *see* "what is" rather than "what isn't."

Saying "thank you" to life strengthens us and sustains us. It is nourishing that part of us that is linked to Universal Energy.

See that the feeling of gratitude drives improved work performance far better and more cost effectively then fear does.

Appreciation opens the door to more common sense/wisdom.

PRESENCE/BEING IN THE MOMENT

Being in the moment introduces you to a new world. Being in the moment connects you to your true identity. This connection brings you peace and contentment. You are no longer a victim of your thoughts, rushing here and there, to the past or to the future, but at peace with the quiet strength inside of you. This state gives you clarity, calmness, and allows insight to emerge. This peace is our birthright.

Just live, enjoy life every moment. That is hope in action.

Coincidence and connectedness directly relates to being in the moment and Universal Mind.

Being in the moment = power, clarity of thought; takes one beyond physical and mental struggle/pain.

Being in the moment is enormously helpful: brings new depth to "being in service," helps you listen better and respond more fully from the unknown. Easier to *see* state of mind and adjust—this lessens having to do damage control.

Being present maximizes wisdom.

Time versus timelessness—only *now* is real and where the answers lie; the rest is illusion.

Noticing when overwhelmed allows one to shift to the present—being in the moment. When you're in the moment, you stop being overwhelmed. Overwhelm comes from futurizing.

Sydney Banks quote: "Beyond time/space/matter." *See* the profundity and practicality of this; being in the moment is a taste of Syd's quote. This affects the quality of listening and thinking.

Being in the moment brings contentment, appreciation, clarity, and the ability to handle whatever comes up.

Staying focused is natural when you live in the moment. Your business will unfold as it is meant to, not necessarily as you think it should.

See beyond time/space/matter—how ordinary this is, yet at the same time, extraordinary. Simply being in the moment, in the zone, not conscious of time, of hunger, thirst, of your body, of space. Just *be.* The more you *see* those moments, the deeper you go into clarity of thought.

Being in the moment offers us fresh ways of communicating.

See beyond complexity to the simplicity of life. Being in the moment is key to keeping life simple.

Learn to appreciate being in the moment, not comparing with other times, but simply enjoying what is in front of us *now.*

Even good memories/good intentions can get in the way. Intention is futurizing. Living is *now.* Sharing is from *now.*

Being in the moment—why is this helpful? It eliminates extraneous thoughts that get in the way of clear thinking. Equally important, being in the moment brings out a deep feeling of caring that draws out mental health in others and then their thinking is clearer.

PAST

When people keep going into the past, they do so from insecurity and lack of true knowledge.

Sometimes it's difficult to let go of past successful procedures or strategies in order to try something new. The familiar saying, "If it's not broke, don't fix it" can be a scapegoat. Check the feeling to see if this is appropriate.

See how prior memories can get in the way of making decisions in the moment, i.e. Elsie's experience of selling previous home in 3 days and therefore expecting to sell current home in 3 days. Memory was wonderful but still got in the way of current situation. Keeping prior memory alive led to expectations—all based on thought.

Subtlety of living in the past, i.e. wanting roll top desk like the one we had before, not being open to new things, not being conscious. Once we open to new things, it helps us to see life with new eyes.

When we continue to harbor ill will toward someone or something that happened in the past, we hurt ourselves. It's like banging our head against a wall and wondering why it hurts.

People move beyond the past via deeper feelings; mental door opens—understanding relieves depression/stress.

Reflect on how we live more in the past *subconsciously* than we are aware of. Like the iceberg, we only see a little of what we do. It is what we *aren't* aware of that will make the difference when that knowledge comes to light.

CONFIDENCE/POTENTIAL

The purpose of life is to understand that, whatever is going on, ultimately we'll be okay. *See* life as an opportunity to uncover and develop our potential.

Much of the world perceives that confidence and humility aren't in partnership, but true confidence and true humility are in complete accord.

"Yes, but..." thinking creates a "Yes, but..." reality, so people don't see the potential they have.

Youngster in juvenile detention didn't see that being calm for an hour was growth on his part. All he could see was that he'd been put in "time-out" when he did have a short period of acting out. However, pointing to his calm left him thoughtful and moved him toward health, and deepened his regard for his potential.

Same applies to employees who think they're just factory workers; so they feel, what can they do in regard to the "big picture"? Help them see the relevance of state of mind on how they view work/life. This will help them see their jobs with pride and confidence and get a taste of their true value.

When individuals are happy, all is right with the world. Family, work, life, all look different from a healthy, confident state of mind.

Cherish the Energy behind life.

EGO

How one offers help to others can either invite acceptance or non-acceptance of the offer. If ego is attached to the offer, it may not be accepted and may create stress, both to the one offering help and to those whom the help is being offered.

Where does ego come from? Personal thinking, self-fabricated imagine of self. What drives ego? Insecurity. *Seeing* this neutralizes judgment and brings compassion.

See with simplicity that we live in security or insecurity. All inappropriate behavior comes from insecurity, based on ego and created by thought.

When we get into ego, we end up defending our personal reality, which is a dream/illusion.

When someone's ego is hooked and defensive, sometimes the best the other party can do is stop, listen, and do damage control. Question to ask, "Will what I offer help or hurt?"

Ego will fight to keep us in our old beliefs. It may take getting used to living in wisdom more of the time. Your analogy of getting used to living in a new house is like getting used to living "inside."

High bar of expectation = ego, which prevents you from *seeing* your own wisdom.

Ego protects self, wisdom promotes Self.

FREE WILL

We have the free will to choose: respect - disrespect, trust - distrust, love - fear, hope - hopeless. It's our choice always; that is what free will offers, the freedom to think what we want.

Interesting how siblings from the same family can have totally different mind sets; one can be hopeful, and one not have much hope. One can live in the past, and one can live in the present. Once again, free will/ choice on how we want to live.

Nothing but good comes from Universal Mind so how come negative stuff happens? It's the marriage between humankind and spiritual reality, between the form/formless. We have the gift of free will to create whatever reality we want; good or bad, and to learn from this. Life is a classroom.

Notice more the flow of thoughts. Realize the difference between positive flow versus stressed flow. i.e. hot/cold faucets. We have the power, via our thinking, to turn off or adjust, when we feel our thoughts getting "hot."

Using our free will via Thought is how we build our world. If we think negative, we will build a negative world. Likewise if we think positive, we will build a positive world—our choice.

We have a choice on what tone/feeling we operate from. Step back, take a breath, be quiet, and *listen.*

Life is about choices—do we want the feeling of patience or impatience? Do we want the feeling of "why them and not me" or the feeling of "I'm lucky to still have a job."

Understanding the phrase "Don't take things personally," means "Don't take those thoughts and make up story." This is great example of free will and choosing wisely...

INNATE MENTAL HEALTH

BEST MEASURE OF healthy functioning is how quickly you return to mental health, after you've visited unhealthy thinking.

People *feel* mental health when in the presence of it because they too are innately health at their core—even if they don't know it.

Wisdom and inner common sense is buoyant and will emerge past our personal thinking. When that happens, it is evidence that innate mental health does exist. When we are in the moment, mental health is most present.

Sometimes it is confusing to people who think that "positive thinking" is what they need to do. It is awareness that we are the thinker that releases healthier thinking, automatically. That is really what innate health is about. It is our default setting, not something we have to consciously "do."

True self-worth is your default setting; all human beings have this capacity. Learn how to release it via insight, as you did when you realized the drama that's been happening is a blessing. This realization moved you forward to discover more about your inner being.

Reflect on the difference between being "taught" to be quiet and "accessing" the calm that is already part of innate mental health.

See how struggling to understand tragic events can lead to anger. Gaining perspective about how we *think* about tragedy can move us past anger into our default setting, innate mental health.

See there is a degree of calmness in you despite the storm.

See beyond personality to innate mental health. Innate health is neutral. Personality changes according to your level of understanding of how the Principles create experience.

The more you understand, the less stress you have. You don't take things personally.

When you *know* you've experienced calmness/mellowness, this is evidence that you already have this capacity within you.

Take time to notice and acknowledge your default setting of mental health. This is very important as it provides more sustainability to your healthy state of mind.

See how "true self" comes out in people. Our true self is innate mental health—everyone has it but not everyone uses it. Some may cover it with faulty thinking. Our true self never goes away—it's always available.

Come back to Self. When you do that, you are loving, gentle, wise and the answers come.

Look inside your own mind—that is the only place you will find the answer to changing the outside reality. Inside your mind is a wealth of resources: strength, incentive and satisfaction in a job well done.

Remember that the nature of thought is pure energy, so it flows. Use thought wisely—let negative thoughts flow out of your mind. Then your natural well-being will rise to the surface.

Consciousness + Neutrality = Innate Health

RELATIONSHIPS

BARB'S INTRO TO RELATIONSHIPS

AT THE HEART of all relationships is connection. You see this theme throughout, as Elsie guides her clients, and their own wisdom comes forward through insight. Reflecting on these nuggets brought another depth of clarity to me.

I used to think that connection took effort. That it was random, elusive at times. That it was something outside of me. But just like the clients in the next pages, the understanding of the Principles has shown me the truth. Connection is innate. I was waiting for connection to happen but then woke up to the fact that it's in me and all around me. I am connected at all times. The only thing that makes me feel separate is my thinking. That's it.

There's a power behind life that if we get in touch with it, it takes us, as Elsie explains, to a depth of feeling that lets us know we are one. Being present to that feeling, our connection includes our presence and the presence of something greater than us. In that, there is no separation.

When I began to see the oneness many new insights opened up for me. Somehow our humanness became more precious. I began to see how we're all in this together. I used to think vulnerability was about a willingness to be weak. Reading the nuggets I realized that instead it's a willingness to be seen.

A surprising outcome has taken place, my compassion naturally sky rocketed, not only for myself but my compassion for others too. Again pointing to what Elsie's clients experienced, that when we reside in wisdom or sit in the certainty of our connection, compassion is natural; we hear more and we understand each other more. Like one of the nuggets suggests, we see beyond the word, find a deeper feeling and a connection.

Seeing this made all my previous ideas about needing to protect myself, or hold back, or be cautious with others, look completely irrelevant. There is nothing to fear – those ideas are just different forms of insecure thought. And when I look in the direction of connection and oneness there is nothing else to do.

In that connection is everything we need. It informs our lives, guides us in the moment and fills us up.

RELATIONSHIPS

LOVE IS CONDITIONAL when we are in a lower state. We expect people to behave in a certain way and judge them or are hurt by their behavior. Take this as a signal that our thinking is off and be grateful for that knowledge.

Insight of having "choice" is powerful and life changing. Insight offers forgiveness of self and others, noticing more positive things versus negative, interacting more positively and compassionately with others, less attachment to hot topics, more understanding and well-being.

To improve relationship: don't focus on problems—focus on innate health/wisdom within each person. This healthy attention brings more clarity on how to solve the problems.

Quality of time in a relationship is more important than quantity of time. Quality of time keeps things fresh and vital, allowing for enjoyment of the simple things in life.

See beyond behavior; when someone is acting out, understand that the behavior is based on beliefs and insecurity, all thought. *Seeing* beyond behavior allows for more understanding and better communication.

When there is no trust in a relationship, you want to pause and reflect on the healthy aspects of your rapport with that individual. This may lift the relationship to another level of understanding allowing for more trust and respect.

Relying on past assessment of individual to decide the future is living in the past and will get in the way of seeing the person now. That's not to say that you would stick your hand in the tiger's cage again....(Sydney Banks' quote) Trust your deeper intelligence on what to do next.

"It's not about making trucks—it's about relationships." Right on! In the same way that "It's not about being right—it's about keeping the feeling positive." is right on. Both are powerful statements.

See beyond behavior, like anger and aggression, to the core of health or wisdom. *Seeing* provides neutrality, and being able to be in service and take care of what needs to be done. This understanding is powerful and has far reaching impact.

COMMUNICATION

Rapport and deep listening are the heart of communication. In the absence of rapport, communication struggles.

Is there value in practicing "word smith" communication, a technique where you prepare what to say in advance? The feeling behind the word is what matters. The feeling will guide you as to what to say and how to say it in the best way possible. Practicing is surface and gets in the way of real connection.

Connection leads to true communication, understanding, deep listening and a genuine interest in what people have to say.

We all operate from either insecurity or security. When someone acts out, they are operating from insecurity. If we react to that, we also are operating from insecurity. The more we *see* this, the more perspective we gain, and the less personally we take things. We can still hold people accountable, but with understanding, not judgment.

See that if you don't view people as "bad feeds," this kinder attitude will make a difference in how you communicate with them. When you don't judge people from a personal state of mind, you have a better chance of a productive conversation.

Look to yourself when the feeling is off in relationships, and ask yourself these questions: "Am I in rapport? Am I listening deeply enough? Am I in service?" All questions NOT aimed at your thinking but aimed at your understanding.

Curiosity comes from wisdom, opening the door to open and honest dialogue. It allows for heart-to-heart conversation. Even if the other individual doesn't respond, you're still in a win-win situation because you're out of the struggle and into wisdom, which allows for healthy functioning.

Secure thinking produces secure feelings. When asking questions from a secure state of mind, the tone will be calm and curious, without agenda. Or there may be no questions at all, just implicit trust and understanding. When asking questions from an insecure state of mind, the tone will be off, with feelings that are perhaps accusatory, judgmental, and so on.

See with fresh eyes that living in a calmer state and being attentive to relationships is a gift that touches others. It allows us to be more present, both at work and home. Sometimes we tend to take our well-being for granted.

"Life is a contact sport," Sydney Banks' quote. Even with understanding you can still get "jabs" but not so intense.

See that it's better to be free of stress than insist you're right.

Relationships and rapport are key elements in communication and knowing how much direction is needed to guide others.

Withdrawing from unhealthy conversation is wisdom in action. Withdrawing allows for healthier thinking to emerge and to re-engage from healthier state of mind.

TAKING THINGS PERSONALLY

STRUGGLE COMES FROM subjective thinking, causing us to take things personally, which leads to assumptions.

When we are out of touch with wisdom, we take things personally.

Slipping in and out of innate mental health is natural; it's human. The trick is not to take that personally! It just is. When you see that fact with neutrality, you rebound quicker.

See that when someone is hurting mentally, their behavior reflects their state of mind. Have the wisdom to not take it personally.

Seeing "psychological innocence" evokes understanding versus judgment.

Not taking things personally when things go wrong offers clarity in terms of resolving what went wrong and then having insights for solutions.

Taking off the "to me" in a sentence helps de-personalize and neutralize the situation. The more we do this, the more clarity of thought we experience.

How to let go of control? Stop, look, *listen* to wisdom when taking things personally. Deep listening helps shift from ego thinking to wise thinking.

What helps you stay out of the drama? Realize that you are experiencing a level of calmness beneath your anxiety because you are operating at a higher level of consciousness, a higher level of functioning. This calmness provides you with the clarity to not lay blame or judge.

Taking things personally = ego = frustration = invested in outcome. All thought.

It's human nature to vent from time to time. When we consistently vent, we are thinking the same thoughts over and over, making them our reality. This affects not only ourselves but those around us. *Seeing* this provides balance.

See that all behavior stems from two modes of thought—secure or insecure. This *seeing* brings understanding and lessens our attachment to others' insecure behavior: arrogance, not listening, insensitivity, and so on.

COMPASSION

COMING FROM THE heart brings compassion and is the best way to help people feel "safe." When people feel safe, they tend to relax and trust others more.

During redundancy situation, keep in mind that the feeling of compassion and respecting the dignity of people will be felt beyond the words you use to separate an employee from the company. Showing up from compassion will help stabilize the situation.

The calmness that you have helps you see with compassion those who are struggling. You know they're hurting mentally, which is why they push others' buttons.

Compassion is balm to a hurting or troubled individual. During times of uncertainty, insecurity and so on, compassion goes a long way in calming troubled waters.

CONNECTION

Deep connection brings deep feelings—connection is the most powerful agent for communication.

Keep in mind that heart-to-heart conversation doesn't involve the technical aspects or details of business. The focus is on the feeling of the interaction and the relationship. Once the feeling in the interaction is healthy then you can deal with the specifics of things.

The buddy system built on empathy versus commiseration is invaluable; helps relieve stress and promotes team work.

Connection is a willingness to bear our soul—vulnerability—Universal Energy in action!

Connectivity: when there is a major shift in spiritual understanding, it affects us all, regardless of where we are in the world.

Don't forget the power of connection; simply by keeping calm and grounded yourself, people will be touched by that "feeling."

Finding a deep feeling, a connection with others from different cultures, brings about commonalities versus differences. This is *seeing* beyond the word.

LISTENING

When you are functioning in your wisdom, you don't need to practice "listening skills;" you naturally listen better because your mind is clear.

Listening beyond the words, to the feeling/essence, gives you more value. This quality of listening comes from inside of you. It connects you to the "real" person inside, soul to soul, heart to heart. This allows you to be more in service, lessens reactivity and judgment, and enhances your relationships. Listening adds more enjoyment to your life and to your work.

Listening with compassion and being silent with understanding is different than just being quiet and still having judgment going on inside your head.

Being sensitive when someone is not feeling listened to, and then listening more deeply, is very impactful. This sensitivity can set an example and prove helpful to others who may not be aware of the value of deep listening.

Listen for relevance without looking for outcome—clears the mind of clutter. In other words, listen for a way to connect to what makes sense to them and build on that.

Listening to your inner wisdom helps you listen more deeply to others, improving communication.

Listening for wisdom automatically puts you in the position of observer and your participation is automatically healthier.

LEADERSHIP

BARB'S INTRO TO LEADERSHIP

Having been an executive in charge of leadership development, employee engagement, learning and organizational culture for a large global company, this section hit home for me on many levels. For years I worked with leaders from around the world, helping them improve their ability to lead, influence and drive change. We would work with them on things like their leadership presence, their communication skills, team effectiveness, etc., basically focusing on skills and competencies.

As Elsie and her clients so clearly demonstrate in each of the following leadership sections, there is something much more powerful at work than our skills, competencies and experience. That's our state of mind. When I saw the relevance of the Principles and state of mind and the role they play in the way leader's lead and organizations struggle or thrive, a whole new world opened up for me.

Simply put: our state of mind trumps any training or model we've been taught. Elsie's clients come to that realization many times in many ways. They share amazing insights where they can see the relationship between their stress and poor decisions or their clarity and new ideas. When they share how they were able to see beyond someone's personality to their wisdom. Or where they were able to listen with compassion versus react. Overall, a theme emerges. . . they are walking around with more ease, in a better feeling and as a result, they are functioning at a much higher level.

"Where we come from" or our "feeling" is more powerful and influential than anything we say. People respond to our feeling not our words. You can see this come to life for the leaders as they share the role they play in creating a healthy work environment, or maintaining a positive tone in meetings and interactions with employees. For example, if a leader walks into a meeting in a low, panicked or angry state of mind, his/her feeling level clearly dilutes whatever message he was trying to get across.

I was also struck again at the theme of "seeing" throughout. Elsie and her clients talk at a very deep level about the gift of seeing inner leadership as equally important as formal leadership, seeing who you really are on the inside; seeing an employee's innate wisdom and helping bring it forward and ultimately seeing that at the heart of a leader's ability to influence is rapport.

I really appreciated reading Elsie's teaching points and the insights of her clients as they began to see more and more clearly the connection between their state of mind, their clarity, their feeling level and their results.

Leadership could be defined in terms of relationship and taught in terms of the capacity to connect with employees and customers, at a deep level.

LEADERSHIP

Primary role of managers/supervisors is to help maintain a mentally healthy environment for their team and ultimately for the company. All technical aspects of the job are enhanced with this healthy mind set.

As a manager, keep in mind that expectations and overly high standards can keep people insecure and feeling bad, therefore preventing the very thing you are wanting; innovation, productive work and a healthy bottom line.

Clear thinking leads to more understanding; enhances the ability to prioritize work, stay on task, and share why this is important with others, in a way that is helpful without being patronizing.

Focus on what people do well at work versus what they've done wrong. Why? This brings out the best in them, accesses their innate mental health so they think more clearly and function at a higher/healthier level.

Look at how inner leadership, in regard to *seeing* who you really are on the "inside," will change the way you lead on the outside.

A calm person will, more often than not, naturally take the lead and direct the situation in terms of leadership.

An important part of leadership is maintaining the positive tone of interactions/meetings/relationships. The optimistic tone/feeling of interactions is what elicits the healthy functioning in others, providing them with insights, creativity, and an opportunity for innovation and change.

Wise leaders make sound decisions based on wisdom/common sense—the feeling that comes from wisdom helps neutralize any tension that may arise from difficult decisions.

If leaders' state of mind remains unclogged by all the details of contingency plan, leaders would be able to come up with appropriate plan when necessary. That's what clear thinking offers!

Making contingency plans, planning for bad behavior, is traditional. That mental position uses up valuable energy making up a story that hasn't even happened! It distracts from true organizational and individual growth. Building on a mental 3 Principles foundation leads to clarity of mind. Clarity can then be applied to specific business goals.

A "wake-up call" given with compassion to an individual who is mentally asleep on the job can be very direct. Sometimes it may cause some grouchiness like a bear woken from hibernation but in the long run it may be necessary for the overall good of the team.

When an individual "tries on" old habits, people can judge and say "there he goes again." What helps in times like this is for the leader to understand it is human to "try on" old habits. That's how we learn that we don't want to be in that state anymore; that's how we grow. When the individual is given some space to ease out of their struggle, chances are they will *see* more clearly and will be able to demonstrate to others that they're okay and have really changed.

As a leader, it's valuable to *see* separate realities—allows us to listen more deeply and understand how the other individuals see life/work.

You are in the leadership role for a reason. You offer your staff and employees more than technical/people skills. You offer a level of wisdom that helps stabilize the whole company, from the corporate level to the plant floor. Keep your head high.

Quiet leadership emerges simply by listening more deeply to your inner wisdom. Deep listening creates "closet geniuses." Sydney Banks' quote.

What is the advantage of *drawing* out of employees versus telling employees? Drawing out provides information on the best way to communicate/relate to one another. Helps employees feel ownership of the project. Telling employees creates dependency. Wisdom provides balance.

Relying on experience and the ability to direct others are wonderful assets. However, they are secondary to *seeing* who people really are at their core. *Seeing* their innate wisdom and the ability to bring that out is primary.

See inner leadership as equally important as formal leadership. Inner leadership is the ability to *see* innate logic/common sense in people beyond their behavior. This draws out common sense versus fanning the flame of frustration, anger, or whatever unproductive behavior may be taking place.

STATE OF MIND

CONSIDER THAT STATE of mind has everything to do with business and with life. State of mind drives beliefs and values structure. A more rigid state would lean toward structure more than an open minded person.

State of mind dictates the kind of assumptions we have. The clearer the state of mind, the less attached we are to assumptions. Less clarity, the more meaning we attach to assumptions.

Improvement in states of mind is driving improvements in the work place. Healthy states of mind allow wisdom to emerge which creates better reality. "Spirits high—moves like a butterfly."

"Weeding the mind" has far reaching results on leadership. A mind free of weeds offers more clarity to see what can be helpful.

How to maintain "vacation state of mind"? Once you've shifted from "outside to inside," trust and faith allow space for innate mental health to emerge.

See that as an individual, we are more than the organization. When we draw on our inner resources, we are sustaining our own mental health. This healthy state of mind contributes to the overall health of the company.

Remind the team how everything is connected, even how the environment around us is affected by our thinking. Even if sometimes we feel we're in a toxic situation, when our state of mind changes, our perspective can shift to understanding and compassion. This shift allows a deeper quality of leadership to emerge.

Why do we caution people not to examine their thinking? Thinking is only one piece of the puzzle. Consciousness plays an equal part in the process. If people aren't aware of the Principle of Consciousness, they are apt to get lost in the content of their thinking. Their state of mind and feeling level gets unhealthy, trying to figure out what thought triggered the behavior/action.

It's more important to know that we produce better when we're in a mentally healthy state than the specifics of why/how. Once employees are relaxed, stress is absent, clarity emerges, and chances are they'll connect the dots that a relaxed clear mind = performance. If not, that's okay too.

Facial expressions/body language are indicators of state of mind—change state, expressions will change. State of mind is the foundation of expression.

Where does mellowness come from? From you or from music or other favorite things? *From you.* Therefore, the mellow/calm state of mind can be available anywhere, at work, at home, riding your horse, flying your plane.

See that state of mind will fluctuate and be okay with that; it's natural. The benefit of *seeing* this is that you catch yourself more of the time when you are about to blow it with a colleague or whomever.

Getting a fresh perspective on value of state of mind—*see* that despite anger and frustration, you bounce back and move forward. This is an example of a healthy state of mind. Way to go!

When you're in healthy state of mind, you won't take things personally if not everyone buys into what you want to do. You will have more balance and understanding.

INFLUENCE

KEEP IN MIND that to have an open and honest communication, it is best to keep a healthy, positive tone in dialogue. Don't focus on barriers; focus on what's positive. At some point, with a positive foundation in place, barriers can be looked at and resolved.

When your spirit or state of mind is light/healthy, the feeling of health draws people and produces good results. It's the partnership of profound and practical.

When environment is less healthy, the best you can do is "keep the feeling alive." This goes beyond the words, beyond the form of the reality. This is being in the moment, grateful for life, for work.

Saying "no" with respect and diplomacy regarding someone's consistent requests and dependence on you can free them up to rely more on their own wisdom.

Hearing nuggets of wisdom from others often opens the door to people having their own insights.

When people tap into their wisdom, their enjoyment and passion for their work is enhanced; consequently the bottom line will be enhanced.

Noticing more neutrality in interacting with others, even when delivering bad news or giving feedback in making changes in the office. This calmness with compassion helps others as well as keeping yourself healthy with a balanced perspective.

Focus on individual's common sense and that quality will emerge. Focus on poor behavior and that will emerge.

Being grounded in calmness helps and offers respite to others. Even if they lose it once you've passed by, that moment of respite is better than adding to their frustration. This is not to be taken lightly.

We can influence others' behavior but can't change their behavior. Only they can change themselves.

Tone of voice comes from tone of thinking. Change thinking and tone of voice changes. However, soft tone without genuine sincerity means nothing. It's dust in the wind.

When an employee is having a hard time, speak to their innate logic versus speaking to their behavior.

Seeing the human spirit in people is what neutralizes your attention on their behavior and provides understanding.

Keep in mind that data stimulates the intellectual thought process. We're discovering that wisdom stimulates original, new thoughts. Therefore leaders who can stimulate employees' wisdom find them more creative and productive and able to use intellect and wisdom in harmony.

Being in the moment helps us *see* beyond the wants/needs of different groups. *Seeing* helps us find common ground to bring about complete accord or at least a degree of alignment.

RAPPORT

THE NEUTRALITY OF rapport takes you beyond personalities, beyond not liking someone because of their behavior. Neutrality is the ability to not take things personally. Neutrality allows you to agree to disagree and still build respect, trust and credibility.

How to motivate employees? Lay foundation of rapport and listen, listen, listen.

Rapport, seeing beyond behavior, to the innate wisdom in people, is what drives every aspect of effective communication/trust. Rapport is a deep feeling that allows for understanding and compassion.

When meetings are moving into dysfunctional behavior, the best antidote is rapport and keeping the tone positive. At the very least, if you stay in the healthy zone, this will offer some balance.

Feelings of rapport come from just being you in a healthy state. People pick up "BS" just as they do sincerity. People respect sincerity and will step on "BS."

Ninety percent of communication is non-verbal. This speaks to the importance of the quality and significant value of rapport in interactions with others.

Why does Principle based rapport work? We are all made up of pure energy. The more we are in tune with that energy, the more it automatically touches others' energy/mental health/rapport.

There are different feelings to rapport: sometimes it feels warm and fuzzy; other times rapport is a feeling of neutrality; and at times rapport can be felt while standing your ground. The common ground is that the tone will be respectful and you will *see* the innate health in people despite their behavior.

When you sense employees or anyone you are interacting with getting edgy, pause and re-establish rapport and listen again.

In order for "inquiry from curiosity" and "seeking to understand" to work, beyond being techniques, you must have a strong foundation of understanding and rapport. Otherwise, it's mere words.

What's most important is rapport; the business goals are secondary. When people feel safe, they think clearer; their ability to listen gets better and then business goals will become clearer and have more chance of being achieved.

When you listen deeply, as you did with the team, you saw and felt the shift in energy. That is the Principles in action, feeling like rapport.

LEADERSHIP PRESENCE

Seeing innate health beyond behavior is inner leadership. In other words, your wisdom is leading rather than ego which tends to focus on behavior. This allows you to remain more consistently in your well-being, and promotes healthy relationships.

Reflect on impact one has on department/company simply by living in a healthy state of mind more of the time. i.e. defusing situation with co-workers by realizing you were creating your own reality. Your co-workers were not responsible, even though it looked like it.

Entrenchment on both sides gets in the way of listening deeply to find alignment. Those who have understanding of how experience is created are challenged to demonstrate good-will and re-listen for relevance.

Interesting to note how "presence" draws out warmth and information, occasionally from the most unlikely person. This shows that people are in touch with wisdom/common sense whether they know it or not. i.e. someone who is on strike sees it as "it is what it is" and lives in that situation with a lot of wisdom, thus defusing stress. This illustrates natural leadership and is inspiring to others.

See value in quiet leadership: the ability to listen without your own thoughts getting in the way, and the ability to draw the best out of your people.

Take a fresh look at what you bring to the table, i.e: level of calmness, clarity, leadership. People notice it, even when you don't. . . when you take a fresh look at the bigger picture of what you offer, this will help you move past your frustration that people aren't seeing as much as they could.

Often times when things get static, it's because people are becoming complacent and unappreciative of their innate health. They may need a gentle nudge toward their wisdom, creativity and leadership from within.

As you grow, your team grows.

As team leader, focus on supporting and reinforcing the mental health of your team. Even if they're venting and stressed, listen for their wisdom and point it out to them. This has the power to bring them back to clarity.

When the shadow of leader is calm, it ripples out and calms others. When the shadow of leader is stressed, it ripples out and stresses others.

ACCOUNTABILITY

Helping people be accountable versus holding people accountable makes a world of difference. Helping is being in service; holding is more a demand.

Tough love from the Three Principles perspective is accountability with compassion.

The difference between "holding" versus "helping" individuals be accountable. Holding = can be punitive. Helping = developing leadership qualities, trust, creativity, innovation, etc. Helping comes from *seeing* innate health.

Another way to *see* the difference between "holding" people accountable versus "helping" people be accountable. Holding = judgment and responsibility. Helping = understanding and pointing to common sense. Helping them feel safe so their state of mind calms and their common sense, in terms of what needs to be done, is accessed.

Know that enhancing employee morale by speaking to and drawing out their wisdom and common sense will help them become more personally responsible, accountable and creative.

When you're feeling mentally healthy, you are in a state of service to your employees and will intuitively know how to reach out.

CHANGE

How to change company culture to more positive? Understanding the Principles releases your wisdom and helps you stay mentally strong. As the leader, this healthy mind set will draw out the health of others. Benefits: employees will be calmer, have better listening, improved morale, more patience; creative and productive which improves the bottom line.

A healthy corporate culture recognizes that accountability and standards are a reflection of common sense and wisdom.

Know that your level of calmness adds a presence of health to the culture of the organization and when you share that presence with others, it touches their innate health and brings about change.

Why is it important to acknowledge healthy change when it occurs? Change awakens peoples' curiosity. Curiosity leads to the question "what prompted the change?" And the conversation begins.

Don't try and change the world. Change your view of the world and the world will change; maybe not in the way you anticipate but in the way the Universe is meant to be.

Be open to change—*see* that in order to change, you need to let go of some of your present beliefs/reality.

Healthy state of mind allows one to flow with organizational changes—that's living in "now."

Healthier organization = healthier production. This change in the organization substantiates the value of preventive maintenance for people; preventive maintenance being the inside-out understanding of the Three Principles.

Small minority in plant can create poor attitude as well as create calm. So you have pockets of calm/sanity and pockets of unrest/insanity. The pockets of calm help stabilize the situation.

What helps change be less stressful and more effective? Quality of feeling and community, "We're all in this together." Optimistic feeling helps to drive vision and helps people feel safe and involved versus feeling stressed.

People can be uncomfortable with change and can use any logic that makes sense to them as to why they don't get it. That's what our thinking does. If we're uncomfortable, it starts with our thoughts.

Change happens—how it's implemented makes all the difference. Speak to the innate wisdom in people—that's how solid relationships are developed and maintained. Relationships are key in meeting the challenges of change.

Patience is required in terms of new managers *seeing* the calmness in some during chaos and not in others. Curiosity and interest may be stirred—how can this person be calm during organized chaos? Then deeper conversation can happen, naturally.

Trust wisdom inside yourself to help you weather change—wisdom provides grounding. Analogy. . . TV is plugged in, just as you are plugged into wisdom. Whether you choose to dial in or not is your decision.

Wisdom helps stabilize critical situations and provides ability to downplay "noise" of organizational changes.

See that if employees at all levels understand the Principles this will help "drive change." When that isn't happening, the best you can do is lead by example; never lose hope that perhaps someone else may be touched by that. At the very least, you lessen your attachment to outcome.

Appreciate that when someone is new to this understanding and still has some insecurity, they tend to "look over their shoulder" at the inside-out nature of experience. That's a good thing. They're still in the ballpark.

STRESS/UNCERTAINTY/CALMNESS

See THAT JUST by being calm yourself, as a leader, helps others by: a) Person that was stressed may later see something of value in what you said. b) You are offering them a moment of respite from stress. c) You didn't fan the flame of their stress.

Even in uncertainty, you can keep mentally healthy when you understand the role of the Principles. Talk about being able to count on something solid! That's what Principles offer.

Goodwill = vaccine = mental protection for people being separated, (made redundant) at least for a time. Better than negative removal where people have not only lost their jobs but lost their feelings of self-esteem.

See the value of your "come from" and how it impacts others when dealing with difficult situations. Coming from an empathetic feeling helps defuse the situation.

Take time to cherish your spirit! Stress is wisdom's way of telling you to slow down and take time for yourself.

How do we face up to an on-going uncertain work environment? It's still our choice how we choose to relate to the story; ultimately, we make up the story. It's working with what is instead of what isn't! It's about how the form changes as the formless, via our thinking, shifts into more positive energy.

How do we thrive versus survive in the midst of stress? Observe and acknowledge common sense and wisdom in yourself, in your team and in executive staff. This acknowledgement reinforces and sustains a healthy state of mind.

When insecurity is in play, our ability to think clearly and respond to questions is not good. Even when the questions to the team are meant to be helpful, they won't be seen that way because the team is currently operating from an insecure state where everything looks like attack.

Judging yourself and others comes from experiencing stress. The moment you *see* where you are living mentally is the moment your stress will start to dissipate.

See the importance of state of mind as it relates to stress; there is a direct correlation. Trust that the more you turn "inside" to your natural wisdom, the more your state of mind will calm.

"Drainers/complainers" drain only if we allow it. *See* them with compassion and then deal directly, with wisdom as your guide.

What is the difference between venting and moving on, versus constantly venting? Wisdom is letting thought flow naturally, as it's meant to do, thereby moving on from stress. Constantly venting is harboring stressful thoughts, hurting ourselves over and over again. Which do you choose?

What is the value of calmness, particularly when in crisis mode? This may seem a simple question but some people think we don't have time for calmness. . . In reality, calmness doesn't have anything to do with time. As a matter of fact, we don't have time NOT to be calm.

Experiencing calmness is a result of less anxious/worrying thoughts—frees mental space for us to think more creatively/insightfully.

TEAM

LAYING THE GROUNDWORK for team development by sharing the Principles may confuse some people who are used to learning via the intellect versus insight. This confusion is natural. However, the Principles aerate mental capacity and allow new thinking to emerge which clears the confusion.

Build the team by a) Listening to them more, not for their complaints but for their common sense. You can preface your meeting with this request. b) Being aware when you are listening to make your point. This means you've stopped listening to what they have to say. c) Staying in rapport; keep the tone or feeling of the meeting positive.

It's best to go for the "high road;" focus on the positive members of the meeting versus paying so much attention to the naysayers. Positive critical mass will ultimately lead the way and help settle the skeptics.

When the dynamics of the team become defensive, it is important to be in integrity to what you see. Standing your ground with compassion and understanding will help defuse the situation. This is an opportunity for "edge" training, meaning taking a stand on tough situations. "Leading edge" is sticking your neck out for what you know.

Focus on what you and your team are doing well, NOT on what is not being done well. This provides more incentive for all to do better and for people to be held accountable, from a state of understanding rather than intimidation. Focusing on what is wrong creates insecurity and poor performance.

See with compassion, not judgment, the difference between teams that are defensive, consumed with change, and worn down—versus teams with good rapport, better relationships and in alignment. Work environment doesn't wear you down when state of mind is healthy.

Coach team about not taking things personally; relate to Thought more rather than hearing too many of their details. When you listen to a lot of detail, it can help make the details real—that is the power of our thinking!

Higher levels of consciousness (*seeing*) bring higher levels of responsibility, with ease.

When you are out of integrity with what you know, you end up stressed. When you maintain your integrity, you maintain your clarity. This helps others works cohesively. i.e. "*see* the team as pistons, each supporting the other."

DISTINCTIONS

BARB'S INTRO TO DISTINCTIONS

So many of these distinctions spoke directly to me. I resonated with much of it and could immediately see and feel the value of looking towards my knowing, my being, and life unfolding. Just reflecting on those words alone settles something down inside of me and simultaneously opens up something new.

In my mind, all of these point me to the difference between the personal self versus the authentic self. Or as Elsie refers to it in one of her books, "Our True Identity."

One of the greatest gifts of this understanding has been the falling away of all my ideas about who I should be, what I should be doing, all my evaluations and assessments about how I'm doing in life and if I'm on track. While I used to think it was a good idea to consider and ponder all those questions, I now see that it was noise in the system and often led to pressure, insecurity and dissatisfaction. Through my understanding of the Principles, I now see those ideas and beliefs as thought. They were my personal self. As that became clearer, their power and significance diminished and was replaced with an inspiration and expansion of myself: my authentic self.

This was a gentle falling away and coming forward and did not require an excavation. Previously, I would have thought I needed to "work on it," overcome my character flaws or my bad habits; but when we let our true nature lead, we see there is absolutely nothing to fix. When we let go, connection to life, to others and to wisdom is a given. As a result, our confidence, our certainty in the power of Mind, our depth and our lives flourish.

DISTINCTIONS

WHAT IS THE difference between wishful thinking and productive/insightful thinking? Wishful thinking comes from the intellect and doesn't promote change. True change is initiated by insight, new thought from Mind. Consciousness is aware of this new thought which produces a shift in understanding resulting in lasting change.

See the difference between Universal Mind power and personal will power. Universal = constant availability of Universal Mind. Personal will = will power from our personal mind that comes and goes according to our level of consciousness.

See the difference between "working" your thoughts versus "observing" your thoughts. Working means consistently analyzing your thoughts. Observing allows you to be more neutral during a rough patch of mental stress, to assess the damage and take time out to repair.

Model wisdom versus teach wisdom. Model means "walking your talk" which demonstrates wisdom. Teach uses words to convey meaning and doesn't necessarily demonstrate.

It's not so much about "lowering our standards" when we observe faulty thinking and don't point it out. It's more that our standards change. Our standards are drawn to point out mental health rather than dysfunction.

What is the difference between *knowing* and believing? *Knowing* comes from Universal Mind. *Knowing* brings certainty, even if not sure of the details. Beliefs come from the intellect and are learned. Beliefs vacillate.

Knowing is before thought—sensing is a degree of *knowing* via experience, i.e. sensing the Principles are spiritual in nature by the deep feeling of connection to Universal Mind and *seeing* the results.

Sometimes the pendulum swings from a level of "It'll be what it'll be" which can be an excuse for just about anything, to "It'll be what it'll be" which means acceptance of what is. Trust the feeling to guide you. You'll know which one is an excuse and which is real.

There is a big difference between "unfolding" versus "working" on something. Unfolding is a natural process that happens when you listen to your wisdom. Working on something is listening only to the intellect.

The difference between: practicing versus realizing. Practicing = intellect, having to <u>do</u> something to release wisdom. Realizing = wisdom, happens naturally. I.e. when you "practice" listening compared to being in your wisdom and naturally listen more deeply, because your mind is calm and uncluttered.

Suggest focus on "that" I think versus "what" I think. Lingering on "what" I think leads to content of thought. Focusing on "that" I think leads to the Principle of Thought.

Reflect on the difference between examining our thoughts versus *creating* our experience. It's the difference between "that we think" versus "what we think". That we think lends itself to neutrality, what we think leads to content and entrenchment.

What is the difference between being *aware* to check-in with your team versus the technique or process of checking in? Aware = Consciousness, natural, *seeing* like radar. Technique = more thinking about thinking.

What is the difference between insight and intellect? Insight = comes from Mind/new thoughts. Intellect = comes from brain, learning by memorization.

See the difference between being aware of behavior and being aware that we *create* behavior. Being aware of behavior can lead to judgment. Being aware that we create behavior leads to understanding.

See the difference between "being me" and "being Me." It's the difference between the personal me and Universal Me.

TEACHING/SHARING WITH OTHERS

BARB'S INTRO TO TEACHING/SHARING WITH OTHERS

For those of you that work in this field, whether you're just starting out or have been at it for a while, you might relate to what I'm about to say. I was deeply touched by the Principles in my own life and immediately I knew I wanted to bring this into my work. I was so excited about it and had a deep knowing that this conversation was the one I wanted to be having with others. I could feel the depth and the hope and the possibility.

My drive, my passion and my desire to be good at this began taking the lead in my learning. I was listening through the filter of, "How will this help my clients?" In a way, I stopped listening for my own growth and deepening, but began trying to see how to apply it to my business or my clients. I would begin to have an insight and rather than letting it sink in, I would immediately go to my intellect and think, "Oh this would be good for so and so", or "How will this help me grow my business?"

It was during a conversation with Elsie that I realized my desire was getting in my way. I had to fire myself from wanting to be a good teacher/coach and deepen my own understanding in the Principles. Elsie talked about residing in wisdom. I could clearly see I wasn't savoring the insight, I was rushing forward and this wasn't serving my clients or me. It was keeping my understanding at a more intellectual level. It comes back to the simple truth that we cannot teach what we don't have.

When I settled down and got quiet, of course, I still wanted to have impact with my clients, but I could see the way I'd been going about it was in the wrong direction. When I stopped trying to be good and just began to listen and learn for my own sake, my learning curve naturally evolved and deepened. My own insights came to life for me in a whole new way. From there, I had more to offer. That journey never ends and I still feel like a newbie.

What this has shown me is the power of this teaching comes exclusively from our ability to connect authentically with others, to have a soul-to-soul connection, and to speak from what we know to be true for ourselves. The feeling is what transfers to others. It's something coming through me versus from me. That feeling sparks something inside of them and their wisdom and intellect begin working together for their lives.

This is true not only for teachers or practitioners but for leaders who want to share with their teams or parents with children or friends with friends, etc. We simply remain curious, stay on our own learning curve, savor our insights and share what we see.

TEACHING/SHARING WITH OTHERS

APPRECIATE THE SENSITIVITY of offering help/sharing the Principles with others, in a way that doesn't infer that there is something wrong with those you are assisting. This sensitivity allows more chance of an open door for them to listen and learn.

Often people are unaware they are showing any wisdom so highlight their nuggets of mental health. This helps shift them to deeper levels of clarity which then assists them to see ways to resolve issues. The more they *see* their own wisdom, the more this sustains well-being.

See beyond behavior to the human spirit. If you talk to the inner core of the person, you get a far better response than if you talk to the behavior.

People change through a shift in their level of consciousness, which then changes behavior. Change happens from the inside-out.

When you're sharing with individuals or groups, listen deeply for natural wisdom. Look for points of alignment, philosophically, not technically.

i.e. an individual was resistant to topic of "insight" and how this can transform life. During a private conversation, he shared that he was a "born again" Christian and how this changed his life. We were in accord that insight and "revelation," his word, were the same. A beautiful feeling sealed the alignment.

Sharing your own story is another way of showing your vulnerability and humanity. It lets people see that, first of all, it's possible for people to change. Not everybody sees that. Many times you will hear someone say, "Oh, that person will never change." *Seeing* someone change gives hope to others.

When you stick to "All's I know is what I know" you can't go wrong. You will find that your ability to articulate your understanding increases the more you *see* that what you know is very profound.

When people are skeptical and think the Principles are "illogical", that is quite common. When people don't understand that we create our reality, it can be hard for them to see what we're seeing. That's why it's essential to "walk our talk" and live in wisdom and common sense as much as we can. People may be skeptical but will still be attracted by how we respond to life.

Support others' mental health by being mentally healthy yourself. Take care of Self and you will continue to thrive.

Help your clients see that many things they are noticing is Consciousness in action. i.e. "Less noise in my head." This is not ego/personal noticing but wisdom noticing.

Bridging the gap between teaching the Principles and what a group wants to intellectually learn involves deep listening. Deep listening provides the bridge between what they know and what you want to offer.

Deep listening brings a quiet ambience which helps others to settle down and activates their innate mental health.

Just show up! The example you shared of being yourself in one of your other projects and having strong impact without even talking about the Principles illustrates the power of your own health touching others at a fundamental level. Trust it more. You'll find your ability to articulate your knowledge will be enhanced.

You see a separation between you and the Principles. When you "just show up" and trust that you will be guided by wisdom then you and the Principles are operating in synch.

Trust the power of the Principles in presenting to new people. The feeling that emerges from you and the audience as you're talking speaks to the fact that they, too, are pure spirit. Trusting this elevates the sharing process. Wisdom is eager to get out.

If you do "listening preparation" with a group or individual before sharing the Principles, it's like putting the form before the formless. Trust that sharing the Principles first will help people listen.

When coaching others who are struggling with chaotic situations, often the best you can do is to listen. Listening in and of itself is healing as it brings out a deep feeling of caring. Just so long as you don't take their issues on yourself! *See* the information simply as information and don't get attached to it. Guide them back to wisdom in terms of where they want to live; in a frustrated state or in peace and harmony.

It is essential to pay attention to the feeling in the room. For example: a teacher becomes student when participant whispers, "My wisdom doesn't feel good." Teacher ignores statement. Silence occurs and feeling in room goes down—results are significant. Teacher finally "hears," re-engages group and wisdom is released to support moving forward.

It's helpful when pointing people in the direction of their own wisdom to also help them recognize the "feeling" they have when they know what's right for them. When our thinking is confused and we are gripped, it is the "feeling" that will alert us to the fact that our thinking is off track.

Sometimes people don't know what they are feeling because they are so caught up in their thinking. Recognizing the difference in feelings points back to Consciousness and our ability to make wise choices.

It's unnecessary to find out what people are insecure about, in the same way that it is irrelevant to view the content of thought. Pointing to the simplicity that we operate from security or insecurity will ultimately show us insecurity is thought.

Explore the nature of the Principles rather than what they do. Why is this important? It's easy to slip into methodology and analysis when exploring what the Principles do. When we focus on the spiritual nature of Principles this takes us to a deeper level of feeling and understanding. It's the difference between form and formless.

See the power of dialogue, coming from wisdom, and the impact this can have on others. There is simplicity and depth that reaches the soul.

If we wait until our life is perfect before we share, we will wait until hell freezes over.

See beyond the words to the essence behind the words. This deep feeling goes a long way in helping people move past uncertainty or apathy.

You don't have to seek to understand what people's thinking is; that process only gets you mired in the content of thought. You simply want to see that they "think." This allows you to be neutral and nonjudgmental. It brings understanding because your own mind in not filled with personal thoughts.

The "feeling" of understanding when sharing with someone, is in and of itself, a healing agent.

LOOKING FOR HEALTH/INCREMENTAL CHANGE/ EVIDENCE OF THE PRINCIPLES

Look for incremental change in people, i.e. a moment of quiet coming from someone you may think isn't hearing anything. That moment of quiet is their intellect coming to a stop and wisdom coming to the forefront. Their intellect may take over again, but that moment of quiet is incremental change.

Why is it helpful to point out incremental change, particularly to someone struggling with a low state of mind? a) Supports confidence b) Helps individual to relax/listen better to their wisdom and others' wisdom c) Lessens blame/judgment d) Increases inquiry/curiosity.

When people are struggling with their stressful thinking, showcase their nuggets of mental health. i.e. "When I gets my mind right, then I'll move ahead;" "Not acting on my thoughts;" "I know it's time for a break;" "I know not to call the office when I'm in a low mood to resign."

Showcasing innate mental health reinforces the fact that health is there, even in the midst of busy thinking. It also gives people respite and a taste of their own wisdom. This lessens the strength of negative thinking.

It's a great service to point out when someone has gained ground. It helps them see themselves and others with less judgement. They are more apt to listen and will come out of their struggle quicker. i.e. individual who is still struggling with relationship is less stressed than he was before. Equally important—the other individual in the relationship is more open to conversation, less contentious, not as angry, and not as withdrawn. Progress is happening.

Being on a plateau is a good thing—it lets you see with perspective. Once you've seen all there is on that plateau, another comes along. This is called "infinity"!

Seeing incremental change helps us be less intense in our desire to see things change more rapidly. Calm is the key to personal advancement.

Even during stressful times, s*ee* that life gives us "continuing education" to help us evolve. Don't judge yourself—BE GENTLE.

So often people will say something that they have no idea is wise or full of common sense. People don't realize they have wisdom and can be deeply touched when they are pointed in this direction.

When one has judgment about a decision but no judgment about decision maker, this is incremental change and significant.

See that core essence transcends the brain. i.e. this applies to one who is stressed to the max and not thinking clearly. They may not be in their health but they "feel." Their core rises to the surface via a "feeling." Help them feel safe!

Acknowledge that YOU made the choice, no matter who helps you on the journey; it's still YOU who made the ultimate choice to move forward. This deeper acknowledgement leads to more wisdom and sustainability.

Reflect more deeply on incremental change. This will help your coaching and help you feel more appreciative. It's "*seeing* what is instead of what isn't." (Syd's quote)

FORMLESS/SPIRITUAL NATURE OF LIFE

BARB'S INTRO TO FORMLESS/SPIRITUAL NATURE OF LIFE

As I read this section and reflect on the 'nature' of the Principles and the spiritual nature of life, a few things occur to me.

Like many of us, I have spent my life looking at the form; my goals, achievements, surroundings, relationships, to determine how I was doing in life.

My focus and attention was mainly in the direction of my wants, likes, dislikes. What does my life look like? What needs to change or improve? Do I like where I live, my job, my social life? What do I want to create in my life and how do I do it? These were the questions that consumed most of my time and energy. The path to happiness was wrapped up in doing more, being a successful woman and having certain things in my life.

In these nuggets you can see that Elsie and her clients challenge us to go deeper; to look beyond the form into the formless nature of life. We are actually limited by the form. By placing our curiosity in the formless we wake up to our true nature, which is infinite potential. As stated in the following pages, "The formless energy is the power".

This shift of attention from the form to the formless continues to be one of the most profound journeys on my path to a deeper understanding. I have so much more to learn and see. I'm incredibly grateful for what has already become clear—even small shifts can lead to great new insights.

By letting go of my wants and my ideas of what success looks like, something deeper inside of me emerges and opens up and guides my life. I begin to touch my "spiritual essence" or my "true nature". And what gets created or comes forth from that deeper place always seems to be beyond what I could have planned or predicted for myself.

More importantly, the feeling it opens up within me adds richness to my life, to my connections with others and fills my life more than any of my achievements or any form ever could. Looking more in the direction of our true nature, our spiritual nature, has allowed me to connect more authentically with people in my life and my clients.

FORMLESS/SPIRITUAL NATURE OF LIFE

See HOW THE deeper dimension of life helps provide a sanctuary from the distractions of our everyday world. When we are more cognizant of this deeper aspect of life we have less attachment to the distractions.

See that the formless energy is the power that drives the intellect/brain.

See the difference between exploring the "nature" of the Principles versus exploring what the Principles "do." S*ee* that focus on "nature" promotes insights versus opinions.

Nature of the Principles is innate/spiritual. When we look at how the Principles work and what they do, we are looking at the form, looking at the pot instead of the clay. We are limited by form. Formless energy is where form comes from, via thought.

Consider the illusionary nature of reality, i.e. reality changes as our thoughts change. Benefit of this knowledge is that we don't remain as gripped by our "reality."

Formless/form and illusion/reality: *See* that as our thinking changes, so does reality; therefore, life is illusion. Reality is only in the moment.

Look at "thought release" connection. Release thought, reality changes. How could reality change unless it is illusion to begin with—pure energy made into form by our thinking.

Remember the inner spirit is stronger than the physical and helps balance the body/life.

Embracing that divine spark within adds stability, happiness and peace of mind.

Presence of a person = spiritual essence.

Self-educate on the true nature of humanity. The more you *see* the spiritual essence of people, beneath the behavior, the less reactive one becomes and lives in more harmony with the world.

The more we see formlessness in action, the less gripped we get by the form.

See the connection between humanity's psychological and spiritual nature. This and the focus on innate mental health versus mental illness is partly why the Three Principles is considered a new paradigm. The main distinction is that for the first time we have an understanding of the foundational Principles underlying the human experience. This is a new era in the field of mental health.

EPILOGUE

THE PREFACE IN this book speaks to the remarkable occurrence of Sydney Banks being invited to consult with the home office of the company he worked for as a welder for many years. To quote what I said: "To say that the invitation was unusual doesn't do justice to this unexpected situation. Syd was an ordinary man, who had continued laboring as a tradesman at the pulp mill for several months after his epiphany; and now here he was, invited to consult with top level executives at the corporate office. How could that be? What drew the executives' interest to meet with a regular workingman, seeking his advice on improving management-employee relations and morale?"

It seems most apropos to end this book with another extraordinary occurrence, featuring a historic event that took place at the Scottish Parliament in Syd's hometown, Edinburgh, Scotland, on May 26, 2015. Sydney Banks' work was the heart of the presentation, entitled: "Tackling Public Health Prevention from the Inside Out." This event was organized by Jacquie Forde, CEO of The Wellbeing Alliance and sponsored by Murdo Fraser MSP. I was honored to present on the panel.

The Wellbeing Alliance are raising the profile of the benefits of the Principles to encourage discussion, debate and a move towards utilizing the Three Principles understanding to improve the mental health and wellbeing of Scotland's citizens via their Wellbeing Academy.

Speaking on the panel at the Parliament meeting in Edinburgh was the most mystical, dream like experience. Syd's muted image was on large screens situated around the meeting room. The screens were setup for a short video clip to be played at the end of the meeting. The clip was of Syd speaking about the power the Principles hold for alleviating humanity's suffering and the potential for bringing peace to the world. With Syd's image in the background, the panel felt his presence, and I for one, was deeply moved by this.

While the feeling was rather dreamlike, nonetheless, the panel spoke in a very down to earth and practical manner. The focus of this meeting was about improving the health and wellbeing of Scotland's citizens. We spoke about the power of a shift in state of mind, from searching outside for solutions to life's challenges, to seeing that inside each person lies a limitless resource of wisdom and guidance, providing the answers humanity seeks.

The panel spoke about this resource being a key element in bringing about sustainable change in individuals, organizations, communities, and countries around the world.

Stories were shared of people who, disillusioned with society, had left their careers to find a simpler life style, thinking this would help them be happy and stress free. From the earliest days of his teaching, Syd was very clear and firm in letting us all know that we *are* society and as such have a responsibility to help, not to abandon the social order.

These same individuals found hope and wisdom that transformed their lives, as their inner health was stirred and awakened. Once again they were able to contribute to their communities, far more than they ever had before, and in doing so, inspiring other citizens to do the same.

One example was of a young attorney who had left his law practice in the city, burned out and disillusioned by life in general. He moved to the island with his young wife, hoping to find peace of mind living a simple, alternative life style. After a difficult time trying a variety of self-help programs to find a way to be happy, the attorney met Syd and through listening to Syd's teachings, discovered his own inner wisdom. In a matter of months, the lawyer returned to his practice, happy and content with his life. Ultimately he became a crown counsel and mentored other attorneys and judges around the country.

One story from thousands of stories; people from all walks of life who have found a way to fulfil their potential, to thrive without stress, with this natural understanding unfolding from the inside-out. Accepting and acknowledging their spiritual birthright.

Accompanying Syd to the first meeting at home office had been beyond my imagination; yet never for a moment did I envision his discovery of the Three Principles being presented at the Scottish Parliament. Following his epiphany, Syd predicted that the Principles he'd uncovered would change the fields of psychology and psychiatry and bring about a complete foundational shift in the mental health field that the world had never before seen. However, I never heard Syd predict this historic event that took place at Parliament. I suspect this presentation was beyond his imagination as well.

Suffice to say, Syd's message of hope and transformation continues to ripple out into the world. Many people know of Syd's extraordinary and significant contributions to the field of mental health and beyond. Only vaguely are they aware of the enormous courage it took for him to give up his private life and his work as a tradesman, which was his only means of support, and totally dedicate the rest of his life to serving others in his quest to bring peace of mind to humanity. I dare say that not many people truly understand the relevance and epic significance of his sharing this gift he discovered: a cure for mental illness.

A quiet, gentle evolution: *Seeing* a new era unfold, not only of practitioners/professionals stepping up to the plate, but the younger population in general, carrying the torch of wisdom, generation to generation; thus changing the world from the inside-out.

I have no words to convey the depth of gratitude I feel to have met and journeyed with an Enlightened man. Such an ordinary yet extraordinary man, who gave the world a magnificent gift of true knowledge that will continue to unfold for centuries to come; for eternity.

Sydney Banks was the epitome of the Three Principles; his ability to enjoy the simple things in life spoke to how it's not how many material possessions one has, what socio-economic background one comes from, nor any educational degree that qualifies one to live a happy, healthy life. It's our ability to live in the moment, in the spiritual essence of our being, that brings joy, peace, and contentment. Syd illustrated that daily.

Syd's ability to rebound in an instant from his human nature to his spiritual nature also exemplified the power of the Principles. This resilience offers such hope to humanity. We're not mere mortals, without the power to break out of our mental prison, a prison of thought. We're spiritual beings living in the physical world, with the power of the Universal energy of all things backing us. As Syd so eloquently said, "In the depth of our souls, we discover our divine inheritance."

RESOURCES

www.sydneybanks.org
Syd's website is archived

www.3phd.net
3 Principles for Human Development, Elsie's website

www.threeprinciplesfoundation.org
Hosts the Three Principles School

Your own wisdom!

ACKNOWLEDGEMENTS

FIRST OF ALL, I want to thank all the people who contributed their "nuggets of wisdom" to this book. Their permission in allowing me to go beyond the norm of traditional coaching to the realm within, where wisdom is found, resulted in many amazing and insightful conversations. Many times, their insights prompted new learning for me. I am exceedingly grateful for their openness, their friendship, and their leadership.

Secondly, I want to thank Barbara Patterson. Her fresh perspective, her depth, her wisdom, and her organizational skills all contributed to the flow of the book. Her enthusiastic response in first reading this material gave me pause and helped me *see* the book with more value. I always knew there was something in these writings that I would one day share, but I must say I rather took it for granted. However, Barb's enthusiasm in sharing what she *saw* in these "nuggets" lit my fire.

I love what Barb has added in her introduction to each section. Again, her fresh perspective and insightful observations brought out a fresh appreciation in me. It's been an absolute joy to work with Barb; I'm honored that we've had this opportunity to work and learn together and to share this journey.

I also want to thank Dicken Bettinger, Jacquie Forde, Michael Neill, and James Layfield for their invaluable suggestions. Their feedback made this a better book. I'm grateful they took the time to review and offer advice.

Jane Tucker has been my editor for several books. I have such respect for her wisdom and her editorial skill. She is utterly committed to helping share the message of Syd's gift to the world and I consider her help invaluable.

Made in the USA
Las Vegas, NV
02 June 2021